ILTS
Science: Chemistry (106) Exam Part 1 of 2
SECRETS

DATE DUE

Study Guide
Your Key to Exam Success

System

Dear Future Exam Success Story:

Congratulations on your purchase of our study guide. Our goal in writing our study guide was to cover the content on the test, as well as provide insight into typical test taking mistakes and how to overcome them.

Standardized tests are a key component of being successful, which only increases the importance of doing well in the high-pressure high-stakes environment of test day. How well you do on this test will have a significant impact on your future, and we have the research and practical advice to help you execute on test day.

The product you're reading now is designed to exploit weaknesses in the test itself, and help you avoid the most common errors test takers frequently make.

How to use this study guide

We don't want to waste your time. Our study guide is fast-paced and fluff-free. We suggest going through it a number of times, as repetition is an important part of learning new information and concepts.

First, read through the study guide completely to get a feel for the content and organization. Read the general success strategies first, and then proceed to the content sections. Each tip has been carefully selected for its effectiveness.

Second, read through the study guide again, and take notes in the margins and highlight those sections where you may have a particular weakness.

Finally, bring the manual with you on test day and study it before the exam begins.

Your success is our success

We would be delighted to hear about your success. Send us an email and tell us your story. Thanks for your business and we wish you continued success.

Sincerely,

Mometrix Test Preparation Team

Need more help? Check out our flashcards at: http://MometrixFlashcards.com/ILTS

TABLE OF CONTENTS

Top 20 Test Taking Tips

1. Carefully follow all the test registration procedures
2. Know the test directions, duration, topics, question types, how many questions
3. Setup a flexible study schedule at least 3-4 weeks before test day
4. Study during the time of day you are most alert, relaxed, and stress free
5. Maximize your learning style; visual learner use visual study aids, auditory learner use auditory study aids
6. Focus on your weakest knowledge base
7. Find a study partner to review with and help clarify questions
8. Practice, practice, practice
9. Get a good night's sleep; don't try to cram the night before the test
10. Eat a well balanced meal
11. Know the exact physical location of the testing site; drive the route to the site prior to test day
12. Bring a set of ear plugs; the testing center could be noisy
13. Wear comfortable, loose fitting, layered clothing to the testing center; prepare for it to be either cold or hot during the test
14. Bring at least 2 current forms of ID to the testing center
15. Arrive to the test early; be prepared to wait and be patient
16. Eliminate the obviously wrong answer choices, then guess the first remaining choice
17. Pace yourself; don't rush, but keep working and move on if you get stuck
18. Maintain a positive attitude even if the test is going poorly
19. Keep your first answer unless you are positive it is wrong
20. Check your work, don't make a careless mistake

Science and Technology

Formulating a problem

The first step in scientific inquiry is to formulate the problem. The problem is basically a question that needs to be answered. The problem or question needs to be specific and testable. The problem needs to be interesting, important, and feasible. To fully investigate a problem, an extended experiment or even a series of experiments will need to be performed. In order to develop an adequate problem, the topic to be investigated should be thoroughly researched and studied. Research should include previous experiments performed on the topic and the latest research information available. The problem will define the goal of the scientific inquiry. Without the problem, the researcher cannot proceed. A specific, testable research problem will enable the researcher to formulate a hypothesis and design an experiment. Once formulated, the problem must be stated in concise terms by either posing a question or making a declarative statement.

Forming and testing a hypothesis

A hypothesis is a prediction of the outcome of a scientific investigation. In order to form a reasonable hypothesis, a significant amount of observation must first be accomplished followed by a valid problem being stated. A good hypothesis should be a prediction, and it must be testable. A good hypothesis should take into account the available background information on the topic, and it must be able to be proven wrong by a valid test. In chemistry, a valid test of a good hypothesis will typically consist of a controlled experiment that has only one variable and several constants. The test should either prove or disprove the hypothesis.

Experimental research is a valid method of testing a hypothesis. An experiment should be very specific. An experiment should have only one independent variable that is being manipulated to test its effect on one dependent variable. All other factors in the experiment should be held constant. If possible, an experiment should have a control group that verifies that the dependent variable is actually dependent on the independent variable. A good experiment should have sufficient trials. Typically, a good experiment will take many days or several weeks with numerous trials, and each trial should be repeated several times. In a good experiment, the results must be repeatable and measurable.

Model, theory, and law

A model is a visual representation that is based on scientific evidence. A model can help scientists attempt to explain information that is difficult to understand or visualize. A model is usually limited to specific conditions. Two examples of models in chemistry are J.J. Thomson's plum pudding model, which represented his view of the atom, and Ernest Rutherford's planetary model of the atom, in which he attempted to explain the way that electrons orbit around the nucleus of an atom.

A theory is an explanation for a pattern that is observed in nature. A theory is supported by scientific evidence and has been verified many times by many different scientists. Two examples of theories in chemistry are the atomic theory of matter and the kinetic theory of matter.

A law is a theory that has been verified multiple times by many researchers over an extended period of time. A theory is accepted to be a valid scientific explanation of a pattern that is observed in nature. Examples of laws in chemistry include the laws of thermodynamics and the gas laws.

Observing, concluding, and comparing

Observing is using the senses (sight, hearing, touch, smell, and taste) to gather information concerning the topic being investigated. An observation is a fact. Observations should be accurate and objective. Observations can be qualitative or quantitative.

Comparing is listing similarities of objects and events, whereas contrasting is listing differences between objects and events. All measurements such as weight, temperature, and pH are forms of comparing.

Concluding should include reevaluating the hypothesis. Specifically, conclusions should state whether or not the results of the experiment support the hypothesis.

Inferring, categorizing, and generalizing

Inferring involves interpreting observations. Inferring attempts to explain why an observation occurred. Observations are generally considered to be facts, but inferences can be correct or incorrect. Inferences can be logical or illogical depending on the observer. A logical inference should make sense based on the information available from the observations.

Categorizing is organizing information into similar categories. Categorizing involves identifying and classifying information into groups and looking for patterns in those groups or categories.

Generalizing consists of making broad statements concerning the relationship between quantities or concepts. A generalization should apply to most situations but typically does not apply to every situation. Generalizing is a way to sort information into meaningful statements that can be transferred to new situations.

Controls

A valid experiment must be carefully controlled. All variables except the one being testing must be carefully maintained. This means that all conditions must be kept exactly the same except for the independent variable. Additionally, a set of data is usually needed for a control group. The control group represents the "normal" state or condition of the variable being manipulated. Controls can be negative or positive. Positive controls are the variables that the researcher expects to have an effect on the outcome of the experiment. A positive control group can be used to verify that an experiment is set up properly. Negative control groups are typically thought of as placebos. A negative control group should verify that a variable has no effect on the outcome of the experiment. The better an experiment is controlled, the more valid the conclusions from that experiment will be.

Identification of variables

Every experiment has several variables; however, only one variable should be purposely changed and tested. This variable is the manipulated or independent variable. As this variable is manipulated or changed, another variable, called the responding or dependent variable, is observed and recorded. All other variables in the experiment must be carefully controlled and are usually referred to as constants. For example, when testing the effect of temperature on solubility of a solute, the independent variable is the temperature, and the dependent variable is the solubility. All other factors in the experiment such as pressure, amount of stirring, type of solvent, type of solute, and particle size of the solute are the constants.

Data collection planning

A valid experiment must be measurable. Data tables should be formed, and meticulous, detailed data should be collected for every trial. First, the researcher must determine exactly what data are needed and why those data are needed. The researcher should know in advance what will be done with those data at the end of the experimental research. The data should be repeatable, reproducible, and accurate. The researcher should be sure that the procedure for data collection will be reliable and consistent. The researcher should validate the measurement system by performing practice tests and making sure that all of the equipment is correctly calibrated and periodically retesting the procedure and equipment to ensure that all data being collected are still valid.

Scientific ideas are subject to change

Scientific ideas are always subject to change. The scientific method includes making observations, forming problems, forming and testing hypotheses, and making conclusions. As new observations are made, new hypotheses are formed. As more accurate methods of testing and better equipment become available, testing hypotheses becomes more and more accurate. Incomplete data, new data, or even improved data may change observations and details previously missed. With technology always changing, new observations are continually being made, leading to new hypotheses and better ways of testing those hypotheses.

Nature and scientific knowledge should be consistent with experimental evidence

The word *science* means knowledge. Science includes knowledge of the natural world. Many scientific fields are divided into categories to study and explain natural phenomena. Observations regarding specific physical evidence are made and then tested. This testing attempts to simulate the observations of nature under controlled conditions. Because natural processes operate in a fairly consistent manner, researchers should be able to identify and predict those patterns.

Reproducibility of scientific knowledge

Scientific knowledge should be reproducible. Researchers working independently should be able to repeat experiments and obtain similar results. These results should be commensurate if the setups and the procedures for the experiments are the same.

Reproducibility is not the same concept as repeatability. Repeatability is the ability of one researcher to perform numerous trials in one experiment using the same equipment resulting in similar results. Reproducibility is the ability of several researchers to replicate successive experiments under the same conditions but in different locations and with different operators and achieve the same results. Reproducibility indicates that the original experiment was not flawed or inadequate. Reproducibility is completely independent of the original research using different equipment and operators.

Using models to illustrate scientific principles

A model is a replica or representation of an object or process. Models can look like the actual objects they represent, or models can simply represent the behavior of an object or system while looking quite different. Types of models vary from actual physical objects such as maps and charts to mathematical equations and computer simulations. In chemistry, several models of the atom have been developed over the years. Students can build models of molecular compounds and ionic compounds. Models demonstrating the concepts of diffusing and osmosis are often used. Deoxyribonucleic acid (DNA) is represented by the double-helix model. Gas molecules are modeled with billiard balls or Ping-Pong balls.

Form and function

The concept of form and function typically fits well with biology. Specifically, the form of an organism or organ is designed in such a way as to perform the required function or functions. For example, red blood cells are designed specifically to perform the function of carrying oxygen. The concept of form and function can also be applied to chemistry. For example, in the area of organic chemistry, carbohydrates, lipids, nucleic acids, and proteins are designed to perform their specific functions. Deoxyribonucleic acid (DNA) and ribonucleic acid (RNA) have different structures that enable them to perform their separate functions. Hundreds of proteins with unique structures have very specific functions in living organisms.

Historical development of the atomic model

In 400 B.C., Democritus called particles of matter "atomos." Aristotle (384–322 B.C.) followed with his view of the four elements of air, earth, water, and fire. Aristotle believed that matter could always be broken into smaller pieces of matter. In 1803, John Dalton proposed the atomic theory, in which he proposed an indestructible atom. In 1897, J.J. Thomson identified the electron in the cathode ray tube, and in 1898, he discovered the proton. Thomson proposed the plum pudding model of the atom, in which the pudding represented the positive portion of the atom and the raisins in the plum pudding represented the electrons dispersed through the positive portion. In 1909, Robert Andrews Millikan determined the unit charge of the electron with his oil drop experiment. In 1911, the nucleus of an atom was discovered using the gold foil experiment at Ernest Rutherford's laboratory. Then Rutherford proposed his planetary model of the atom. Later, he proposed the existence of the neutron. In 1932, James Chadwick discovered the neutron.

Impact of the atomic theory of matter

John Dalton's atomic theory of matter is the basis for modern chemistry and physics. Dalton's atomic theory of matter established the atom as an actual physical object with specific properties by replacing Democritus's simple view of the existence of the atom with several well-defined postulates concerning matter and the behavior of atoms. In addition, the atomic theory of matter explained the law of definite composition and the law of multiple proportions. The atomic theory also led to the discovery of the fundamental forces, the quantum theory of light, and Albert Einstein's theory of relativity. The major premises of Dalton's model of the atom are still valid. However, some of the postulates have been modified due to later discoveries. For example, Dalton stated that atoms are indivisible, but today we know that atoms may be split in a nuclear reaction.

Historical development of the gas laws

In 1662, Robert Boyle created an air pump that led to the development of Boyle's law, which describes the inverse relationship between pressure and volume at constant temperature and number of moles. In 1783, Jacques Charles worked with balloons to develop Charles's law, which describes the direct relationship between volume and temperature at a constant pressure and number of moles. Combining Boyle's law and Charles's law yields the combined gas law, which shows the direct relationship between pressure and temperature at a constant volume. The combined gas law has no official founder. In 1802, Joseph Louis Gay-Lussac studied hydrogen and oxygen gas, which led to the development of Gay-Lussac's law, which states that the ratio of the volumes of gases in a chemical reaction are small whole numbers. In 1811, Amedeo Avogadro studied Gay-Lussac's work and published Avogadro's law, which states that equal volumes of gases at the same temperature and pressure contain equal numbers of moles. In 1834, Benoît Paul Émile Clapeyron combined Boyle's law, Charles's law, and Avogadro's law and was the first to state the ideal gas law.

Wöhler's synthesis of urea

Friedrich Wöhler's accidental synthesis of urea in 1828 is considered to be the starting point of modern organic chemistry. At this time, many scientists believed in a concept called vitalism. This was basically a theory that life, including living organisms such as plants and animals, was not subject to the laws of physics and chemistry. According to vitalism, an unknown force or "vital force" governed living organisms. Because of this false belief, scientists thought the chemicals that were found in a living organism were completely different than other chemicals. Scientists believed that these chemicals could not be made artificially. But then, Wöhler accidentally made urea crystals in the laboratory when attempting to synthesize ammonium cyanate. Wöhler was extremely disappointed because he truly had believed in vitalism, but his accidental synthesis of human urea disproved the concept of vitalism. His work brought forward a new understanding of life. Today, numerous complex organic compounds are synthesized or made artificially.

History and development of the periodic table

In the 1820s, Johann Wolfgang Döbereiner grouped elements with similar properties in triads, or groups of three. In the1860s, A.E. Beguyer de Chancourtois arranged the elements by atomic weights in a spiral showing similar elements at regular intervals. Also in the 1860s, John Alexander Reina Newlands introduced the law of octaves. When Newlands arranged the elements by increasing atomic masses, he noticed that similar properties repeated every eighth element. Later in the 1860s, Julius Lothar Meyer and Dmitri Ivanovich Mendeleev independently developed similar periodic tables of the elements arranged by the atomic masses. Mendeleev's periodic table was published first. Mendeleev

- 6 -

correctly placed elements in groups, even moving elements out of the order of their atomic masses to keep them in groups with similar physical properties. Mendeleev also predicted the existence of elements not yet discovered. In the early 1900s, Henry Moseley showed that the elements should be arranged by atomic number instead of atomic mass. This corrected the seemingly out of order arrangement of Mendeleev. In the 1930s and 1940s, Glenn T. Seaborg discovered the transuranium elements and redesigned the periodic table with the lanthanide series and the actinide series being placed below the rest of the elements.

Historical development of the quantum theory of light

Before the development of the quantum theory of light, two contrasting theories of light were presented. The wave theory of light described light as electromagnetic waves, and Isaac Newton's particle or "corpuscular" theory of light stated that light was a stream of particles. In the early 1900s, Max Planck introduced the concept of the quantum while studying blackbody radiation. Planck was able to determine the relationship between the quanta of energy related to the frequency of light and determine Planck's constant. Albert Einstein followed using Planck's quantum concept to explain the photoelectric effect and showed that the energy of an electron depends of the frequency of the electron. Later, Niels Bohr refuted Rutherford's planetary model with the Bohr model with fixed orbits at specific energy levels. In 1924, Louis Victor de Broglie stated that particles exhibit the properties of waves. This was later verified experimentally. Erwin Schrödinger was able to develop an equation to show the properties of the electron in the hydrogen atom that later led to Wolfgang Pauli proposing the exclusion principle in 1925. In 1927, Werner Heisenberg proposed the uncertainty principle, which states that the position and momentum of small subatomic particles cannot be determined simultaneously.

Life Science

Cells in living organisms

The functions of plant and animal cells vary greatly, and the functions of different cells within a single organism can also be vastly different. Animal and plant cells are similar in structure in that they are eukaryotic, which means they contain a nucleus. The nucleus is a round structure that controls the activities of the cell and contains chromosomes. Both types of cells have cell membranes, cytoplasm, vacuoles, and other structures. The main difference between the two is that plant cells have a cell wall made of cellulose that can handle high levels of pressure within the cell, which can occur when liquid enters a plant cell. Plant cells have chloroplasts that are used during the process of photosynthesis, which is the conversion of sunlight into food. Plant cells usually have one large vacuole, whereas animal cells can have many smaller ones. Plant cells have a regular shape, while the shapes of animal cell can vary.

Nuclear parts of a cell

Nucleus (pl. nuclei): This is a small structure that contains the chromosomes and regulates the DNA of a cell. The nucleus is the defining structure of eukaryotic cells, and all eukaryotic cells have a nucleus. The nucleus is responsible for the passing on of genetic traits between generations. The nucleus contains a nuclear envelope, nucleoplasm, a nucleolus, nuclear pores, chromatin, and ribosomes.

Chromosomes: These are highly condensed, threadlike rods of DNA. Short for deoxyribonucleic acid, DNA is the genetic material that stores information about the plant or animal.

Chromatin: This consists of the DNA and protein that make up chromosomes.
Nucleolus (nucleole): This structure contained within the nucleus consists of protein. It is small, round, does not have a membrane, is involved in protein synthesis, and synthesizes and stores RNA (ribonucleic acid).

Nuclear envelope: This encloses the structures of the nucleus. It consists of inner and outer membranes made of lipids.

Nuclear pores: These are involved in the exchange of material between the nucleus and the cytoplasm.

Nucleoplasm: This is the liquid within the nucleus, and is similar to cytoplasm.

Cell structure

Ribosomes: Ribosomes are involved in synthesizing proteins from amino acids. They are numerous, making up about one quarter of the cell. Some cells contain thousands of ribosome. Some are mobile and some are embedded in the rough endoplasmic reticulum.

Golgi complex (Golgi apparatus): This is involved in synthesizing materials such as proteins that are transported out of the cell. It is located near the nucleus and consists of layers of membranes.

Vacuoles: These are sacs used for storage, digestion, and waste removal. There is one large vacuole in plant cells. Animal cells have small, sometimes numerous vacuoles.

Vesicle: This is a small organelle within a cell. It has a membrane and performs varying functions, including moving materials within a cell.
Cytoskeleton: This consists of microtubules that help shape and support the cell.

Microtubules: These are part of the cytoskeleton and help support the cell. They are made of protein.

Cytosol: This is the liquid material in the cell. It is mostly water, but also contains some floating molecules.

Cytoplasm: This is a general term that refers to cytosol and the substructures (organelles) found within the plasma membrane, but not within the nucleus.

Cell membrane (plasma membrane): This defines the cell by acting as a barrier. It helps keeps cytoplasm in and substances located outside the cell out. It also determines what is allowed to enter and exit the cell.

Endoplasmic reticulum: The two types of endoplasmic reticulum are rough (has ribosomes on the surface) and smooth (does not have ribosomes on the surface). It is a tubular network that comprises the transport system of a cell. It is fused to the nuclear membrane and extends through the cytoplasm to the cell membrane.

Mitochondrion (pl. mitochondria): These cell structures vary in terms of size and quantity. Some cells may have one mitochondrion, while others have thousands. This structure performs various functions such as generating ATP, and is also involved in cell growth and death. Mitochondria contain their own DNA that is separate from that contained in the nucleus.

Plant cell structure

Cell wall: Made of cellulose and composed of numerous layers, the cell wall provides plants with a sturdy barrier that can hold fluid within the cell. The cell wall surrounds the cell membrane.

Chloroplast: This is a specialized organelle that plant cells use for photosynthesis, which is the process plants use to create food energy from sunlight. Chloroplasts contain chlorophyll, which has a green color.

Plastid: This is a membrane-bound organelle found in plant cells that is used to make chemical compounds and store food. It can also contain pigments used during photosynthesis. Plastids can develop into more specialized structures such as chloroplasts, chromoplasts (make and hold yellow and orange pigments), amyloplasts (store starch), and leucoplasts (lack pigments, but can become differentiated).

Plasmodesmata (sing. plasmodesma): These are channels between the cell walls of plant cells that allow for transport between cells.

Animal cell structure

Centrosome: This is comprised of the pair of centrioles located at right angles to each other and surrounded by protein. The centrosome is involved in mitosis and the cell cycle.

Centriole: These are cylinder-shaped structures near the nucleus that are involved in cellular division. Each cylinder consists of nine groups of three microtubules. Centrioles occur in pairs.

Lysosome: This digests proteins, lipids, and carbohydrates, and also transports undigested substances to the cell membrane so they can be removed. The shape of a lysosome depends on the material being transported.

Cilia (singular: cilium): These are appendages extending from the surface of the cell, the movement of which causes the cell to move. They can also result in fluid being moved by the cell.

Flagella: These are tail-like structures on cells that use whip-like movements to help the cell move. They are similar to cilia, but are usually longer and not as numerous. A cell usually only has one or a few flagella.

Eukaryotic and prokaryotic cells

The main difference between eukaryotic and prokaryotic cells is that eukaryotic cells have a nucleus and prokaryotic cells do not. Eukaryotic cells are considered more complex, while prokaryotic cells are smaller and simpler. Eukaryotic cells have membrane-bound organelles that perform various functions and contribute to the complexity of these types of cells. Prokaryotic cells do not contain membrane-bound organelles. In prokaryotic cells, the genetic material (DNA) is not contained within a membrane-bound nucleus. Instead, it aggregates in the cytoplasm in a nucleoid. In eukaryotic cells, DNA is mostly contained in chromosomes in the nucleus, although there is some DNA in mitochondria and chloroplasts. Prokaryotic cells usually divide by binary fission and are haploid. Eukaryotic cells divide by mitosis and are diploid. Prokaryotic structures include plasmids, ribosomes, cytoplasm, a cytoskeleton, granules of nutritional substances, a plasma membrane, flagella, and a few others. They are single-celled organisms. Bacteria are prokaryotic cells.

Plant and animal cell differences

Plant cells can be much larger than animal cells, ranging from 10 to 100 micrometers. Animal cells are 10 to 30 micrometers in size. Plant cells can have much larger vacuoles that occupy a large portion of the cell. They also have cell walls, which are thick barriers consisting of protein and sugars. Animal cells lack cell walls. Chloroplasts in plants that perform photosynthesis absorb sunlight and convert it into energy. Mitochondria produce energy from food in animal cells. Plant and animal cells are both eukaryotic, meaning they contain a nucleus. Both plant and animal cells duplicate genetic material, separate it, and then divide in half to reproduce. Plant cells build a cell plate between the two new cells, while animal cells make a cleavage furrow and pinch in half. Microtubules are components of the cytoskeleton in both plant and animal cells. Microtubule organizing centers (MTOCs) make microtubules in plant cells, while centrioles make microtubules in animal cells.

Meiosis

Meiosis has the same phases as mitosis, but they happen twice. In addition, different events occur during some phases of meiosis than mitosis. The events that occur during the first phase of meiosis are interphase (I), prophase (I), metaphase (I), anaphase (I), telophase (I), and cytokinesis (I). During this first phase of meiosis, chromosomes cross over, genetic material is exchanged, and tetrads of four chromatids are formed. The nuclear membrane dissolves. Homologous pairs of chromatids are separated and travel to different poles. At this point, there has been one cell division resulting in two cells. Each cell goes through a second cell division, which consists of prophase (II), metaphase (II), anaphase (II), telophase (II), and cytokinesis (II). The result is four daughter cells with different sets of chromosomes. The daughter cells are haploid, which means they contain half the genetic material of the parent cell. The second phase of meiosis is similar to the process of mitosis. Meiosis encourages genetic diversity.

Mitosis

Interphase: The cell prepares for division by replicating its genetic and cytoplasmic material. Interphase can be further divided into G_1, S, and G_2.

Prophase: The chromatin thickens into chromosomes and the nuclear membrane begins to disintegrate. Pairs of centrioles move to opposite sides of the cell and spindle fibers begin to form. The mitotic spindle, formed from cytoskeleton parts, moves chromosomes around within the cell.

Metaphase: The spindle moves to the center of the cell and chromosome pairs align along the center of the spindle structure.

Anaphase: The pairs of chromosomes, called sisters, begin to pull apart, and may bend. When they are separated, they are called daughter chromosomes. Grooves appear in the cell membrane.

Telophase: The spindle disintegrates, the nuclear membranes reform, and the chromosomes revert to chromatin. In animal cells, the membrane is pinched. In plant cells, a new cell wall begins to form.

Cytokinesis: This is the physical splitting of the cell (including the cytoplasm) into two cells. Some believe this occurs following telophase. Others say it occurs from anaphase, as the cell begins to furrow, through telophase, when the cell actually splits into two.

Cancerous cells

In cancerous cells, the DNA or gene structure is disrupted. Abnormal numbers of chromosomes can develop. Cancer cells can have defective Krebs cycles, and get most of their energy from glycolysis rather than the Krebs cycle. Normal cells get about 70% of their energy from the Krebs cycle and about 20% from glycolysis. In addition, normal cells

- 11 -

usually use oxygen during energy production, while cancer cells mainly produce energy without using oxygen. Cancerous cells lack a blood vessel system and use amino acids to construct it, while normal cells have a built-in blood vessel system. Cancer cells over populate and are very active, making more demands on system resources. The enzymes and hormones involved with cancer cells tend to be overactive or underactive, which can lead to other problems.

Cell theory

The basic tenets of cell theory are that all living things are made up of cells and that cell are the basic units of life. Cell theory has evolved over time and is subject to interpretation. The development of cell theory is attributed to Matthias Schleiden and Theodor Schwann, who developed the theory in the early 1800s. Early cell theory was comprised of four statements: all organisms (living things) are made of cells; new cells are formed from pre-existing cells; all cells are similar; and cells are the most basic units of life. Other concepts related to classic and modern cell theory include statements such as: cells provide the basic units of functionality and structure in living things; cells are both distinct stand-alone units and basic building blocks; energy flow occurs within cells; cells contain genetic information in the form of DNA; and all cells consist of mostly the same chemicals.

Enzymes

Enzymes can be divided into six classes: oxidoreductase, transferase, hydrolase, lyase, isomerase, and ligase. These classes end with the suffix "ase," which is true of most enzymes. Each enzyme catalyzes a chemical reaction. Oxidoreductase enzymes catalyze oxidation reduction (redox) reactions, during which hydrogen and oxygen are gained or lost. Examples include cytochrome oxidase, lactate, and dehydrogenase. Transferase enzymes catalyze the transfer of functional groups, such as the amino or phosphate group. Examples include acetate kinase and alanine deaminase. Hydrolase enzymes break chemical bonds by using water. Examples include lipase and sucrase. Lyase enzymes break chemical bonds or remove groups of atoms without using water. Examples include oxalate decarboxylase and isocitrate lyase. Isomerase enzymes catalyze the rearrangement of atoms within a molecule. Examples include glucose-phosphate isomerase and alanine racemase. Ligase enzymes join two molecules by forming a bond between atoms. Examples of ligases are acetyl-CoA synthetase and DNA ligase.

Metabolism, macromolecules, metabolic pathways, anabolic and catabolic reactions

Metabolism is all of the chemical reactions that take place within a living organism. These chemical changes convert nutrients to energy and macromolecules. Macromolecules are large and complex, and play an important role in cell structure and function. Metabolic pathways refer to a series of reactions in which the product of one reaction is the substrate for the next. These pathways are dependent upon enzymes that act as catalysts. An anabolic reaction is one that builds larger and more complex molecules (macromolecules) from smaller ones. Catabolic reactions are the opposite. Larger molecules are broken down into smaller, simpler molecules. Catabolic reactions release energy, while anabolic ones require energy. The four basic organic macromolecules produced by anabolic reactions are carbohydrates (polysaccharides), nucleic acids, proteins, and lipids. The four basic building blocks involved in catabolic reactions are monosaccharides (glucose), amino acids, fatty acids (glycerol), and nucleotides.

Catabolism

Catabolism is the biosynthetic process by which macromolecules are broken down into smaller molecules. During this process, both energy and molecules that are used in anabolic processes are produced. Hydrolysis is a process used in catabolism. The four main groups of molecules produced through catabolism are monosaccharides (glucose), amino acids, fatty acids (glycerol), and nucleotides. Carbohydrates (polysaccharides) are broken down into sugars or glucose. It is the oxidation of carbohydrates that provides the cells with most of their energy. Glucose can be further broken down by respiration or fermentation by glycolysis. The first step of glycolysis breaks down pyruvic acid with the byproducts of NADH and ATP. Pyruvic acid can then be used in the Krebs cycle or in fermentation. Glycolysis occurs in the cytoplasm of eukaryotic cells. Fatty acids are long chains that are oxidized to acetyl-CoA, which provides energy to cells. Nucleic acids consist of nucleotides. Nucleotide triphosphates such as ATP carry energy. They also release energy when their bonds are broken.

Anabolism

Anabolism is a form of biosynthesis. It usually involves a series of steps, or pathways, where the product of one reaction is used in the next. Anabolism uses smaller molecules to build carbohydrates (polysaccharides), nucleic acids, amino acids and proteins, and lipids. Energy is used and stored during this process. Anabolic reactions can form a variety of macromolecules. An example of polysaccharide biosynthesis in animals and bacteria is glycolysis, the formation of glycogen from glucose with covalent bonds. Examples of nucleic acid synthesis include the formation of DNA, RNA, ATP, and other macromolecules. It can be achieved by either the pentose phosphate or Entner Doudoroff pathways. Protein biosynthesis uses amino acids, which are intermediate products of the Krebs cycle. Lipid biosynthesis uses fatty acids, which are formed from acetyl CoA (coenzyme A) during the Krebs cycle, and glycerol, which is derived from dihydroxyacetone phosphate and glycolysis.

Proteins

Proteins are macromolecules formed from amino acids. They are polypeptides, which consist of many (10 to 100) peptides linked together. The peptide connections are the result of condensation reactions. A condensation reaction results in a loss of water when two molecules are joined together. A hydrolysis reaction is the opposite of a condensation reaction. During hydrolysis, water is added. -H is added to one of the smaller molecules and OH is added to another molecule being formed. A peptide is a compound of two or more amino acids. Amino acids are formed by the partial hydrolysis of protein, which forms an amide bond. This partial hydrolysis involves an amine group and a carboxylic acid. In the carbon chain of amino acids, there is a carboxylic acid group (-COOH), an amine group (-NH_2), a central carbon atom between them with an attached hydrogen, and an attached "R" group (side chain), which is different for different amino acids. It is the "R" group that determines the properties of the protein.

Types of proteins

Alkyl: This is a nonpolar group that forms hydrophobic amino acids. Amino acids include glycine with a single hydrogen atom R group, alanine with a methyl R group, and valine with an isopropyl R group. Leucine and isoleucine also have alkyl side chains.

Hydroxyl: This is a polar group that forms hydrophilic amino acids such as serine and threonine.
Sulfur: Amino acids in this group include cysteine and methionine.

Carboxylic acid: In proteins belonging to this group, a second carboxylic acid group is attached as the R group. This acid group is polar and can be negatively charged when the acidic proton attaches to a water molecule, which leaves a negatively charged carboxylate ion. Proteins that belong to this group include aspartic acid and glutamic acid.

Amide: The formula for amides is -$CONH_2$. Proteins belonging to this group include glutamine and asparagine.

Amino: This group includes lysine, arginine, and histidine. The double-bonded nitrogen atom can take a proton to become positively charged.

Aromatic: This group has a ring structure, and includes the proteins phenylalanine, tyrosine, and tryptophan. Tyrosine is polar, while tryptophan and phenylalanine are nonpolar.

Looped: This group includes praline. Because it is nonpolar, it forms a ring rather than a chain.

Chemiosmosis and enzymes

Chemiosmosis is a process by which energy is made available for ADP to form ATP. When electrons move down the electron transport chain, the energy pumps protons to one side of a membrane. The equilibrium is disrupted at this point because the concentration gradient where the protons have gathered is greater than the concentration gradient on the other side of the membrane. The protons diffuse through the membrane as a result. The energy of this process fuels phosphorylation.

Enzymes act as catalysts by lowering the activation energy necessary for a reaction. They are proteins, have specific functions, are often globular and 3-D in form, and have names that end in "-ase." An enzyme has an active site where a substrate attaches and products are formed and released. Most enzymes also need a non-protein coenzyme that attaches to the enzyme to form the active site.

Nucleic acids

Nucleic acids are macromolecules that are composed of nucleotides. Hydrolysis is a reaction in which water is broken down into hydrogen cations (H or H^+) and hydroxide anions (OH or OH^-). This is part of the process by which nucleic acids are broken down by enzymes to produce shorter strings of RNA and DNA (oligonucleotides). Oligonucleotides are broken down into smaller sugar nitrogenous units called nucleosides. These can be digested by

- 14 -

cells since the sugar is divided from the nitrogenous base. This, in turn, leads to the formation of the five types of nitrogenous bases, sugars, and the preliminary substances involved in the synthesis of new RNA and DNA. DNA and RNA have a double helix shape. Macromolecular nucleic acid polymers, such as RNA and DNA, are formed from nucleotides, which are monomeric units joined by phosphodiester bonds. Cells require energy in the form of ATP to synthesize proteins from amino acids and replicate DNA. Nitrogen fixation is used to synthesize nucleotides for DNA and amino acids for proteins. Nitrogen fixation uses the enzyme nitrogenase in the reduction of dinitrogen gas (N_2) to ammonia (NH_3). Nucleic acids store information and energy and are also important catalysts. It is the RNA that catalyzes the transfer of DNA genetic information into protein coded information. ATP is an RNA nucleotide. Nucleotides are used to form the nucleic acids. Nucleotides are made of a five carbon sugar, such as ribose or deoxyribose, a nitrogenous base, and one or more phosphates. Nucleotides consisting of more than one phosphate can also store energy in their bonds.

Lipids

Carbohydrates, proteins, and nucleic acids are groups of macromolecules that are polymers. Lipids are not long polymers with high molecular weights. They are hydrophobic, meaning they do not bond well with water or mix well with water solutions. Lipids have numerous C-H bonds. In this way, they are similar to hydrocarbons (substances consisting only of carbon and hydrogen).The major roles of lipids include energy storage and structural functions. Examples of lipids include fats, phospholipids, steroids, and waxes. Fats are made of long chains of fatty acids (three fatty acids bound to a glycerol). Fatty acids are chains with reduced carbon at one end and a carboxylic acid group at the other. An example is soap, which contains the sodium salts of free fatty acids. Phospholipids are lipids that have a phosphate group rather than a fatty acid. Glycerides are another type of lipid. Examples of glycerides are fat and oil. Glycerides are formed from fatty acids and glycerol (a type of alcohol).

Catabolization of macromolecules

Amino acids are catabolized either during glycolysis or during the Krebs cycle. First, they are broken down into substances that can be catabolized. Processes used to break down amino acids include transamination, which is the transfer of NH_2 (amine), decarboxylation, which is the loss of -COOH groups, and dehydrogenation of H_2. While sugars like glucose from carbohydrates usually begin to be broken down by glycolysis at the beginning of the cycle, eventually going through the Krebs cycle and then the electron transport chain, proteins get broken down into amino acids and have many different entry points into the cycles. Carbohydrates are responsible for providing energy. They are involved in the metabolic energy cycles of photosynthesis and respiration. Structurally, carbohydrates usually take the form of some variation of CH_2O. In respiration, glucose is completely dismantled, but is only partially broken up during fermentation. Lipids get broken down into glycerol for glycolysis and fatty acids enter at the Krebs cycle.

Glycolysis

In glycolysis, glucose is converted into pyruvate and energy stored in ATP bonds is released. Glycolysis can involve various pathways. Various intermediates are produced that are used in other processes, and the pyruvic acid produced by glycolysis can be further used for respiration by the Krebs cycle or in fermentation. Glycolysis occurs in both aerobic and anaerobic organisms. Oxidation of molecules produces reduced coenzymes, such as NADH. The coenzymes relocate hydrogens to the electron transport chain. The proton is transported through the cell membrane and the electron is transported down the chain by proteins. At the end of the chain, water is formed when the final acceptor releases two electrons that combine with oxygen. The protons are pumped back into the cell or organelle by the ATP synthase enzyme, which uses energy produced to add a phosphate to ADP to form ATP. The proton motive force is produced by the protons being moved across the membrane.

Intermediaries of glycolysis

Glycolysis can involve different metabolic pathways. The following 10 steps are based on the Embden-Meyerhof pathway, in which glucose is the starting product and pyruvic acid is the final product. Two molecules of ATP and two of NADH are the products of this process. To start, enzymes utilize ATP to form glucose-6-phosphate. The glucose-6 is converted to fructose-6-phosphate. Another ATP molecule and an enzyme are used to convert fructose-6-phosphate to fructose-1,6-disphosphate. Both dihydroxyacetone phosphate (DHAP) and glyceraldehyde-3-phosphate are formed from fructose-1,6-disphosphate. It is during the preceding reactions that energy is conserved or gained. NAD conversions to NADH molecules and phosphate influx result in 1,3-diphosphoglceric acid. Then, two ADP molecules are phosphorized into ATP molecules, resulting in 3-phosphoglyceric acid, which reforms into 2-phosphoglyceric acid. At this point, water is produced as a product and phosphoenolpyruvic acid is formed. Another set of ADP molecules are phosphorized into ATP molecules. Pyruvic acid is the end result.

Glycolic pathways

Glycolysis is a general term for the conversion of glucose into pyruvate.

Embden-Meyerhof pathway: This is a type of glycolysis in which one molecule of glucose becomes two ATP and two NADH molecules. Pyruvic acid (two pyruvate molecules) is the end product.

Entner-Doudoroff pathway: This is a type of glycolysis in which one glucose molecule forms into one molecule of ATP and two of NADPH, which are used for other reactions. The end product is two pyruvate molecules.

Pentose Phosphate pathway: Also known as the hexose monophosphate shunt, this is a type of glycolysis in which one glucose molecule produces one ATP and two NADPH molecules. Five carbon sugars are metabolized during this reaction. Glucose is broken down into ribose, ribulose, and xylose, which are used during glycolysis and during the Calvin (or Calvin-Benson) cycle to create nucleotides, nucleic acids, and amino acids.

Monosaccharides, disaccharides, starches

The simple sugars can be grouped into monosaccharides (glucose, fructose, and galactose) and disaccharides. These are both types of carbohydrates. Monosaccharides have one monomer of sugar and disaccharides have two. Monosaccharides (CH_2O) have one carbon for every water molecule. Aldose and ketose are monosaccharides with a carbonyl (=O, double bonded oxygen to carbon) functional group. The difference between aldose and ketose is that the carbonyl group in aldose is connected at an end carbon and the carbonyl group in ketose is connected at a middle carbon. Glucose is a monosaccharide containing six carbons, making it a hexose and an aldose. A disaccharide is formed from two monosaccharides with a glycosidic link. Examples include two glucoses forming a maltose, a glucose and a galactose forming a lactose, and a glucose and a fructose forming a sucrose. A starch is a polysaccharide consisting only of glucose monomers. Examples are amylose, amylopectin, and glycogen.

Krebs cycle

The Krebs cycle is also called the citric acid cycle or the tricarboxylic acid cycle (TCA). It is a catabolic pathway in which the bonds of glucose and occasionally fats or lipids are broken down and reformed into ATP. It is a respiration process that uses oxygen and produces carbon dioxide, water, and ATP. Cells require energy from ATP to synthesize proteins from amino acids and replicate DNA. The cycle is acetyl CoA, citric acid, isocitric acid, ketoglutaric acid (products are amino acids and CO_2), succinyl CoA, succinic acid, fumaric acid, malic acid, and oxaloacetic acid. One of the products of the Krebs cycle is NADH, which is then used in the electron chain transport system to manufacture ATP. From glycolysis, pyruvate is oxidized in a step linking to the Krebs cycle. After the Krebs cycle, NADH and succinate are oxidized in the electron transport chain.

Fermentation

Fermentation is an anaerobic reaction in which glucose is only partially broken down. It releases energy through the oxidation of sugars or other types of organic molecules. Oxygen is sometimes involved, but not always. It is different from respiration in that it uses neither the Krebs cycle nor the electron transport chain and the final electron acceptor is an organic molecule. It uses substrate-level phosphorylation to form ATP. NAD^+ is reduced to NADH and NADH further reduces pyruvic acid to various end products. Fermentation can lead to excess waste products and is less efficient than aerobic respiration. Homolactic fermentation refers to lactic acid fermentation in which the sugars are converted to lactic acid only (there is one end product). In heterolactic fermentation, the sugars are converted to a range of products.

Electron transport chain

The electron transport chain is part of phosphorylation, whereby electrons are transported from enzyme to enzyme until they reach a final acceptor. The electron transport chain includes a series of oxidizing and reducing molecules involved in the release of energy. In redox reactions, electrons are removed from a substrate (oxidative) and H^+ (protons) can also be simultaneously removed. A substrate gains electrons during reduction. For example, when glucose is oxidated, electrons are lost and energy is released. There are enzymes in the membranes of mitochondria. The electrons are carried from one enzyme to another by a co-enzyme. Protons are also released to the other side of the membrane. For example, FAD and $FADH_2$ are used in oxidative phosphorylation. FAD is reduced to $FADH_2$. Electrons are stored there and then sent onward, and the $FADH_2$ becomes FAD again. In aerobic respiration, the final electron acceptor is O_2. In anaerobic respiration, it is something other than O_2.

Homeostasis and feedback loops

Homeostasis is the ability and tendency of an organism, cell, or body to adjust to environmental changes to maintain equilibrium. One way an organism, such as a human body, can maintain homeostasis is through the release of hormones. Some hormones work in pairs. When a condition reaches an upper limit, a hormone is released to correct the condition. When a condition reaches the other end of the spectrum, another hormone is released. Hormones that work in this way are termed antagonistic. Insulin and glucagon are a pair of antagonistic hormones that help regulate the level of glucagon in the blood. Positive feedback loops actually tend to destabilize systems by increasing changes. A negative feedback loop acts to make a system more stable by buffering changes.

Examples of fermentation

Examples of organisms (fermentors) and their products include lactic acid fermentation, whereby streptococcus and lactobacillus bacteria form an end product of lactic acid. Lactic acid can be broken down by propionibacterium freudenreichii into propionic acid and carbon dioxide. This process is involved in making Swiss cheese. Yeast (saccharomyces) and some bacteria produce ethanol during alcohol fermentation, which is commonly used in baking bread and brewing alcohol. Carbon dioxide is also a product of alcohol fermentation. Alcohol fermentation is also involved in making beer. The starter is a malt extract, the fermentor is Saccharomyces cerevisiae, and the end product is ethanol. Citric acid is used as a flavoring. It starts as molasses, which is fermented by aspergillus (a fungus). Lactic acid is found as an end product of fermentation in cheese, yogurt, rye bread, and other foods.

Examples of homeostasis

The hormones insulin and glucagon (an antagonistic pair of hormones) are involved in negative feedback loops in the liver's control of blood sugar levels. Alpha cells secrete glucagon when the concentration of blood glucose decreases. Glucagon is broken down and fatty acids and amino acids are converted to glucose. Once there is more glucose, glucagon secretion is reduced. Beta cells secrete insulin when the concentration of blood glucose increases. This leads to the liver absorbing glucose. Glucose is converted to glycogen, and fat and the concentration of glucose decrease. Insulin production is then reduced. Hormones work in other ways aside from antagonistically. For example, follicle stimulating hormone (FSH) increases the production of estrogen. Once estrogen reaches a certain level, it suppresses FSH production. In some cases, a single hormone can increase or decrease the level of a substance.

Hybrid zygote abnormality: This is when two species produce a zygote that does not survive to birth or germination, does not develop normally or reach sexual maturity, and cannot reproduce.

Allopatric speciation: This refers to speciation that occurs because of geographical factors, such as physical barriers or dispersal.

Sympatric speciation: This refers to speciation that happens within parent populations.

Parapatric speciation: This refers to speciation that occurs because of an extreme change in habitat.

Bottleneck and adaptive radiation

Bottleneck: This occurs when a small percentage of a population survives a disaster or when the size of a population is greatly reduced for at least one generation. It results in reduced allele diversity, and can even lead to entire alleles being eliminated in a species. This can lead to an increased inability to adapt to certain environmental factors. An example of a bottleneck is that hunting by humans reduced the northern elephant seal population to 20 individuals. Their population is now about 30,000, but the population's genes are much less varied than the genes of the southern elephant seal population. Another example is that a typhoon killed all but 30 people on an island in the South Pacific. One of the survivors had the recessive gene for color blindness. Currently, about 10% of the current population of 2,000 is color blind.

Adaptive radiation: This refers to the fact that speciation occurs through adapting to an environment through natural selection. It also refers to the fact that a species has a common ancestor.

Genetic drift and the founder's effect

Genetic drift: Easily observable in small populations, genetic drift is a change in the frequency of an allele.

Founder's effect: This occurs when a small population breaks away from a larger population and forms a smaller and isolated population. The resulting reduction in allele diversity leads to a greater expression of certain genetic traits than would be observed in a larger population. An example is the Amish in America, who are the descendants of 30 Swiss founders. The Amish are isolated by culture and breed within their population. One of the founders had Ellis-van Creveld syndrome. It is rare in larger populations, but is found at a rate of about 1 in 200 in the Amish community. It results in short stature, extra fingers and toes, and heart defects.

Earth's age, abiotic synthesis and endosymbiotic theory

Earth's age is estimated to be 4.5 billion years.

Abiotic synthesis: This is related to the commonly accepted theory that life originated from inorganic matter. It refers to the making of organic molecules outside of a living body, and is believed to have been the first step in the development of life on Earth. The theory was tested in an experiment performed by a graduate student at Stanford University in 1953. He combined the inorganic molecules water, hydrogen, methane, and ammonia in a closed, sterile flask and applied heat. To recreate the effect of lightning, he used an electric charge. His ingredients started as a clear mixture. After a week, he had a cloudy soup that contained amino acids and organic compounds.

Endosymbiotic theory: This is the belief that eukaryotes (cells with nuclei) developed from prokaryotic cells (those without nuclei). The theory is that chloroplasts in plant cells and mitochondria in animal cells evolved from smaller prokaryotes living within larger prokaryotes.

Origin of life on Earth

One theory of how life originated on Earth is that life developed from nonliving materials. The first stage of this transformation happened when abiotic (nonliving) synthesis took place, which is the formation of monomers like amino acids and nucleotides. Next, monomers joined together to create polymers such as proteins and nucleic acids. These polymers are then believed to have formed into protobionts. The last stage was the development of the process of heredity. Supporters of this theory believe that RNA was the first genetic material. Another theory postulates that hereditary systems came about before the origination of nucleic acids. Another theory is that life, or the precursors for it, were transported to Earth from a meteorite or other object from space. There is no real evidence to support this theory.

Five kingdom classification system

The groupings in the five kingdom classification system are kingdom, phylum/division, class, order, family, genus, and species. A memory aid for this is: King Phillip Came Over For Good Soup. The five kingdoms are Monera, Protista, Fungi, Plantae, and Animalia. The kingdom is the top level classification in this system. Below that are the following groupings: phylum, class, order, family, genus, and species. The Monera kingdom includes about 10,000 known species of prokaryotes, such as bacteria and cyanobacteria. Members of this kingdom can be unicellular organisms or colonies. The next four kingdoms consist of eukaryotes. The Protista kingdom includes about 250,000 species of unicellular protozoans and unicellular and multicellular algae. The Fungi kingdom includes about 100,000 species. A recently introduced system of classification includes a three domain grouping above kingdom. The domain groupings are Archaea, Bacteria (which both consist of prokaryotes), and Eukarya, which include eukaryotes. According to the five kingdom classification system, humans are: kingdom Animalia, phylum Chordata, subphylum Vertebrata, class Mammalia, order Primate, family Hominidae, genus Homo, and species Sapiens.

Protista kingdom

Organisms in the Protista kingdom are classified according to their methods of locomotion, their methods of reproduction, and how they get their nutrients. Protists can move by the use of a flagellum, cilia, or pseudopod. Flagellates have flagellum, which are long tails or whip-like structures that are rotated to help the protist move. Ciliates use cilia, which are smaller hair-like structures on the exterior of a cell that wiggle to help move the surrounding matter. Amoeboids use pseudopodia to move. Bacteria reproduce either sexually or asexually. Binary fission is a form of asexual reproduction whereby bacteria divide in half to produce two new organisms that are clones of the parent. In sexual reproduction, genetic material is exchanged. When kingdom members are categorized according to how they obtain nutrients, the three types of protists are photosynthetic, consumers, and saprophytes. Photosynthetic protists convert sunlight into energy. Organisms that use photosynthesis are considered producers. Consumers, also known as heterotrophs, eat or consume other organisms. Saprophytes consume dead or decaying substances.

Fungi kingdom

Mycology is the study of fungi. The Fungi kingdom includes about 100,000 species. They are further delineated as mushrooms, yeasts, molds, rusts, mildews, stinkhorns, puffballs, and truffles. Fungi are characterized by cell walls that have chitin, a long chain polymer carbohydrate. Fungi are different from species in the Plant kingdom, which have cell walls consisting of cellulose. Fungi are thought to have evolved from a single ancestor. Although they are often thought of as a type of plant, they are more similar to animals than plants. Fungi are typically small and numerous, and have a diverse morphology among species. They can have bright red cups and be orange jellylike masses, and their shapes can resemble golf balls, bird nests with eggs, starfish, parasols, and male genitalia. Some members of the stinkhorn family emit odors similar to dog scat to attract flies that help transport spores that are involved in reproduction. Fungi of this family are also consumed by humans.

Molecular oxygen

When the Earth was formed, the atmosphere did not contain oxygen. It is thought to have appeared in the Paleoproterozoic era about 2.5 to 1.6 billion years ago. First, oxygen combined with iron in oceans to form banded iron formations (thin layers of iron oxides and layers of iron poor rock). After that, oxygen began to "gas out" of the oceans slowly. One of the major events in Earth's geologic history is the great oxygen event, or oxygen catastrophe, during which large amounts of oxygen led to the extinction of anaerobic organisms. This, in turn, led to an increased number of aerobic organisms. Eventually, it also resulted in the development of eukaryotic cells and more complex life forms.

Organism and microbe

An organism is a living thing. A unicellular organism is an organism that has only one cell. Examples of unicellular organisms are bacteria and paramecium. A multicellular organism is one that consists of many cells. Humans are a good example. By some estimates, the human body is made up of billions of cells. Others think the human body has more than 75 trillion cells.

The term microbe refers to small organisms that are only visible through a microscope. Examples include viruses, bacteria, fungi, and protozoa. Microbes are also referred to as microorganisms, and it is these that are studied by microbiologists. Bacteria can be rod shaped, round (cocci), or spiral (spirilla). These shapes are used to differentiate among types of bacteria. Bacteria can be identified by staining them. This particular type of stain is called a gram stain. If bacteria are gram-positive, they absorb the stain and become purple. If bacteria are gram-negative, they do not absorb the stain and become a pinkish color.

Viruses

Some scientists do not consider viruses to belong to any of the five kingdoms or to be living organisms for many reasons. Viruses do not meet the definition of a cell. They cannot be classified as eukaryotic or prokaryotic. They are generally smaller than and not as complex as living cells, which are the basic units of life. Viruses do not have nuclei. They are macromolecules consisting of long chains of genetic material (either RNA or DNA) encased in protein. Viruses also lack membrane-bound organelles, ribosomes, and cytoplasm, all of which are usually found in cells. Viruses do not perform the basic cell processes involved in the ADP/ATP cycle, and they are not capable of cellular respiration or gas exchange. They reproduce by gaining control of a host cell and making it replicate the viral DNA instead of its own.

Characteristics of viruses

Viruses are microorganisms that replicate in the cells of other organisms, including plants, animals, bacteria, and other microorganisms. All viruses have a head. Some also have a tail consisting of protein. The tail is used to attach to a host cell and enter it. This is one way in which viruses introduce their genetic material to the host. The head of a virus, also called a protein capsid, contains genetic material in the form of DNA, RNA, or enzymes. The adenovirus and the herpes virus are both DNA viruses. The HIV retrovirus, influenza, and the rotavirus are RNA viruses. The number of virus types is thought to be in the millions. Virology is a branch of microbiology that is devoted to the study of viruses. Viruses can be transmitted to other organisms in a number of ways, such as by insects, by air, and through direct contact.

Vascular and nonvascular plants

Vascular plants have vascular tissue in the form of xylem and phloem. These make up the parts of the plants, such as the roots, stems, and leaves that are involved in transporting minerals and water throughout the plant. This capability enables vascular plants to grow tall. Food/energy that is converted by photosynthesis in the leaves is brought down to the roots, while water is brought to the top of the plant. Nonvascular (or avascular) plants lack true leaves, stems, and roots. Nonvascular plants do not develop vascular tissue, such as xylem and phloem. They tend to be small, and individual cells are adjacent to their environment.

Plant kingdom groupings

Only plants in the division bryophyta (mosses and liverworts) are nonvascular, which means they do not have xylem to transport water. All of the plants in the remaining divisions are vascular, meaning they have true roots, stems, leaves, and xylem. Pteridophytes are plants that use spores and not seeds to reproduce. They include the following divisions: Psilophyta (whisk fern), Lycophyta (club mosses), Sphenophyta (horsetails), and Pterophyta (ferns). Spermatophytes are plants that use seeds to reproduce. Included in this category are gymnosperms, which are flowerless plants that use naked seeds, and angiosperms, which are flowering plants that contain seeds in or on a fruit. Gymnosperms include the following divisions: cycadophyta (cycads), ginkgophyta (maidenhair tree), gnetophyta (ephedra and welwitschia), and coniferophyta (which includes pinophyta conifers). Angiosperms comprise the division anthophyta (flowering plants).

Plant phyla

Chlorophyta are green algae. Bryophyta are nonvascular mosses and liverworts. They have root-like parts called rhizoids. Since they do not have the vascular structures to transport water, they live in moist environments. Lycophyta are club mosses. They are vascular plants. They use spores and need water to reproduce. Equisetopsida (sphenophyta) are horsetails. Like lycophyta, they need water to reproduce with spores. They have rhizoids and needle-like leaves. The pteridophytes (filicopsida) are ferns. They have stems (rhizomes). Spermatopsida are the seed plants. Gymnosperms are a conifer, which means they have cones with seeds that are used in reproduction. Plants with seeds require less water. Cycadophyta are cone-bearing and look like palms. Gnetophyta are plants that live in the desert. Coniferophyta are pine trees, and have both cones and needles. Ginkgophyta are ginkos. Anthophyta is the division with the largest number of plant species, and includes flowering plants with true seeds.

Processes and systems of plants

Plants are autotrophs, which mean they make their own food. In a sense, they are self sufficient. Three major processes used by plants are photosynthesis, transpiration, and respiration. Photosynthesis involves using sunlight to make food for plants. Transpiration evaporates water out of plants. Respiration is the utilization of food that was produced during photosynthesis.

Two major systems in plants are the shoot and the root system. The shoot system includes leaves, buds, and stems. It also includes the flowers and fruits in flowering plants. The shoot system is located above the ground. The root system is the component of the plant that is underground, and includes roots, tubers, and rhizomes. Meristems form plant cells by mitosis. Cells then differentiate into cell types to form the three types of plant tissues, which are dermal, ground, and vascular. Dermal refers to tissues that form the covering or outer layer of a plant. Ground tissues consist of parenchyma, collenchyma, and/or sclerenchyma cells.

Plant transpiration

The rate of transpiration is affected by light, temperature, humidity, wind, and the saturation of the soil. Light encourages stomata to open, and water is lost more quickly than in the dark. Since water evaporates quicker in higher temperatures, the rate of transpiration increases as the temperature increases. If an area is humid, the rate of transpiration is decreased. The opposite is true for areas of lower humidity. This is explained by the principle of diffusion. The greater the difference in humidity or concentrations of substances in two regions, the greater the rate of diffusion between them will be. Water in the soil replaces water that has been lost through transpiration. If water in the soil is not replaced, the rate of transpiration decreases. Photosynthesis also slows, the stomata close, and the plant wilts when it loses turgor as water is lost from cells.

Plant alternation of generations

Alternation of generations refers to the fact that the two processes used during sexual reproduction alternate. These processes are meiosis and fertilization. In meiosis, sex cells divide and genetic material is reduced by half, which results in a gamete. Two gametes are joined during fertilization, and the resulting cell is diploid. This occurs in both plants and animals. Plants have a gametophyte and a sporophyte generation. The gametophyte generation starts with the production of a haploid spore. More haploid spores are produced through mitosis. Sexual reproduction occurs during this stage, which results in a zygote. This is the start of the second generation, which is known as the sporophyte generation. A primary difference between plant and animal sexual reproduction is that plants can undergo mitosis with haploid cells. Cells can be controlled with this single set of chromosomes.

Plant root system

Plant roots include zones where cell differentiation, elongation and division, and meristem formation occur. Primary meristems include protoderms, ground meristems, procambiums, and apical meristems. There is also a root cap. A tuber is an underground stem that is enlarged and used for food storage. A rhizome is an underground stem of sorts that sends out roots and shoots from its nodes (bulging or swelling points). Vascular tissues include xylem and phloem. Xylem can be scattered throughout a pith or formed into rings. Phloem allows for food transport down a plant. The food travels from where it was produced through photosynthesis to other structures, such as roots, that require the food. Phloem can be made up of bundles of sieve tubes. It is usually located outside the xylem.

Meristems in vegetative growth

The meristems of plants are where new cells are formed through mitosis. These cells then differentiate into specific tissue types, which may form part of the root system or increase a plant's girth, height, or length. Cambiums are meristems that are responsible for secondary growth, which increases girth. Flowering plants go through cycles of vegetative growth, or propagation. They use flowers to reproduce sexually. Vegetative propagation occurs at the apical meristems located on the tip of the stem. These start as undifferentiated cells that can form into more stems, leaves, and secondary meristems (or lateral buds), which form branches. Nodes are areas where leaves can develop. The area between nodes is termed internodal. On a stem, the apical meristem on the end is the terminal bud. Sometimes, this can become a flower bud. Lenticels allow for the diffusion of oxygen and carbon dioxide gas.

Transpiration, respiration, and phylogenetic

Transpiration is the movement of water through a vascular plant. It is also the method by which water is evaporated out of plants. Transpiration mainly happens during the process of photosynthesis, when water and minerals travel up through the xylem and are used and water is released through stomata (flattened oval-shaped openings). During transpiration, water is drawn up a plant. This process also helps cool leaves.

Respiration: This refers to the process of metabolizing sugars to provide plants with the energy they need for growth and reproduction. The chemical equation is $C_6H_{12}O_6 + 6O_2 \rightarrow 6CO_2 + 6H_2O + energy$. During the process of respiration, sugars are burned, energy is released, oxygen is used, and water and carbon dioxide are produced. Respiration can occur as a light or dark reaction.

Phylogenetic: This refers to organisms that are related because of their evolutionary history.

Reproduction in flowering plants

There are at least 230,000 species of flowering plants. They represent about 90 percent of all plants. Angiosperms have a sexual reproduction phase that includes flowering. When growing plants, one may think they develop in the following order: seeds, growth, flowers, and fruit. The reproductive cycle has the following order: flowers, fruit, and seeds. In other words, seeds are the products of successful reproduction. The colors and scents of flowers serve to attract pollinators. Flowers and other plants can also be pollinated by wind. When a pollen grain meets the ovule and is successfully fertilized, the ovule develops into a seed. A seed consists of three parts: the embryo, the endosperm, and a seed coat. The embryo is a small plant that has started to develop, but this development is paused. Germination is when the embryo starts to grow again. The endosperm consists of proteins, carbohydrates, or fats. It typically serves as a food source for the embryo. The seed coat provides protection from disease, insects, and water.

Reproduction methods

Bryophytes are seedless plants. They include liverworts, hornworts, and mosses. They use spores that form into gametophytes to reproduce. Sperm are flagellated, meaning they require at least some water to swim to the egg. Some bryophytes are plants that are one sex or the other, but other bryophytes have both sexes on the same plant. Ferns also have flagellated sperm and require water for the same reason as bryophytes. Both ferns and bryophytes undergo alternation of generations. These plants spend about half of their reproductive cycles as sporophytes, making haploid spores through meiosis during this stage. The other half of the cycle is spent as a haploid gametophyte. At this point, male and female gametes join to form one zygote. Seed plants use seeds to reproduce. Flowering plants use flowers and seeds.

Pollination in flowering plants

The anthers of the stamens (male parts) have microsporangia that form into a pollen grain, which consists of a small germ cell within a larger cell. The pollen grain is released and lands on a stigma (female) portion of the pistil. It grows a pollen tube the length of the style and ends up at the ovule. The pollen grain releases the sperm and fertilization occurs. In double fertilization, one of the sperm joins with the egg to become a diploid zygote. The other sperm becomes the endosperm nucleus. Seeds are formed. One cotyledon (monocot) or two cotyledons (dicot) also form to store food and surround the embryo. Correspondingly, monocots produce one seed leaf, while dicots produce two. The seed matures and becomes dormant, and fruits typically form.

Sexual parts of flowering plants

Flowering plants can be categorized sexually according to which organs they have. Flowers can be bisexual or unisexual. Species can be dioecious, which means male and female flowers are contained on different individual plants. Monoecious means that both male and female flowers are on one individual. Bisexual flowers are those that have all of the following: sepal, petal, stamen, and pistil. If they have all of these parts, they are considered complete. They have both the male stamen and the female counterpart, the pistil. Unisexual flowers only have a pistil or a stamen, not both. Incomplete flowers do not have all four parts. The flower rests upon a pedicel and is contained with the receptacle. The carpal is made up of the stigma at the tip, a style, and the ovary at the base. The ovary contains the ovules (eggs). Carpels are sometimes formed as a single pistil. The stamen includes the anther and the filament, and produces the male pollen.

Photoperiodism

Photoperiodism refers to the fact that plants are affected by seasons, particularly by the amount of daylight that occurs in each season. The amount of daylight triggers processes such as flowering, growth in roots and stems, and leaves falling off of trees. Long day plants, like the name implies, do not need many night time hours to instigate flowering. Short day plants have an affinity for longer nights and shorter days. Short day plants tend to flower as days get shorter. Long day plants tend to flower when days get longer. Other plants are considered to be day neutral. Examples of long day obligate (meaning long days are essential) plants are oats, clover, and carnations. Examples of long day facultative (meaning long days are desirable, but not essential) plants are turnip, lettuce, wheat, and barley. Examples of short day obligate plants are tobacco, strawberries, and coffee. Examples of short day facultative plants are cotton, sugar cane, and rice.

Fruits in flowering plants

The fruit can encase the mature seed, such as in tomatoes, cherries, and apples. The seed can also be on the outside of the fruit, such as in corn and strawberries. These are called simple fruits, and are produced by one ovary. Another classification of simple fruits is botanical fruits, which are fruits that develop out of a flower. Examples of these are tomatoes, squash, and eggplant. Simple fruits can also have fruits that are dry. Examples of this are poppies, peanuts, and walnuts. Many nuts are simple fruits formed when the ovary wall hardens. One of the seeds produced remains attached. Aggregate fruits are produced by many ovaries in one flower. Each ovary is separately fertilized and forms the aggregate fruit. Examples of these are raspberries, blackberries, and strawberries. Multiple fruits refer to many flowers on a single structure. Examples are pineapples and figs.

Monocot and dicot structures

The diversity of plants leads to an abundance of plant structures. Not all structures are found in all plants, and many plants have different structures that perform similar functions. Monocots and dicots are both flowering plants. The bark of a woody dicot (tree) is structurally very different than the exterior rind of a monocot corn stem, even though both serve as the outermost layer. Within both are the vascular tissues phloem and xylem. In a woody dicot, the tree trunk is made of xylem. When water is abundant, such as during the spring, the xylem vessels that are made are large. Those made later in the summer are narrower since there is less water. When viewed in cross section, these two layers form the ring of a tree's trunk, which is why they can be used to calculate a tree's age.

Tropism, geotropic, plagiotropic, phototropism, and thigmotropism

Tropism refers to the fact that plants grow in response to specific stimuli. Seeds are geotropic (or gravitropic), meaning they grow as a response to gravity. Roots are positively geotropic and grow towards gravity. Stems are negatively geotropic and grow away from the force of gravity. A seed planted upside down will still grow roots and stems in the right direction. Plagiotropic refers to the fact that secondary branches and roots grow at right angles to gravity. Phototropism refers to the fact that a plant bends or grows toward a light source. Thigmotropism refers to how plants respond to contact. Plant hormones are organic compounds that usually influence changes in plants. They can cause fruit to ripen or instigate plant growth. Five major groups of hormones are auxins, gibberellins, ethylenes, cytokinins, and abscisic acids. Auxins occur naturally and can be synthesized. They affect plant cell elongation, apical dominance, and rooting. Gibberellins affect plant height. Ethylenes help fruit ripen. Cytokinins are involved in cell division. Abscisic acids inhibit other hormones.

Animal kingdom subdivisions

The animal kingdom includes about one million species. Metazoans are multicellular animals. Food is ingested and enters a mesoderm-lined coelom (body cavity). Phylum porifera and coelenterate are exceptions. The taxonomy of animals involves grouping them into phyla according to body symmetry and plan, as well as the presence of or lack of segmentation. The more complex phyla that have a coelom and a digestive system are further classified as protostomes or deuterostomes according to blastula development. In protostomes, the blastula's blastopore (opening) forms a mouth. In deuterostomes, the blastopore forms an anus. Taxonomy schemes vary, but there are about 36 phyla of animals. The corresponding term for plants at this level is division. The most notable phyla include chordata, mollusca, porifera, cnidaria, platyhelminthes, nematoda, annelida, arthropoda, and echinodermata, which account for about 96 percent of all animal species.

Animal kingdom facts

The animal kingdom is comprised of more than one million species in about 30 divisions (the plant kingdom uses the term phyla). There about 800,000 species of insects alone, representing half of all animal species. The characteristics that distinguish members of the animal kingdom from members of other kingdoms are that they are multicellular, are heterotrophic, reproduce sexually (there are some exceptions), have cells that do not contain cell walls or photosynthetic pigments, can move at some stage of life, and can rapidly respond to the environment as a result of specialized tissues like nerve and muscle. Heterotrophic refers to the method of getting energy by eating food that has energy releasing substances. Plants, on the other hand, are autotrophs, which mean they make their own energy. During reproduction, animals have a diploid embryo in the blastula stage. This structure is unique to animals. The blastula resembles a fluid-filled ball.

Animal protostomic

Members of the protostomic phyla have mouths that are formed from blastopores.

Mollusca: Classes include bivalvia (organisms with two shells, such as clams, mussels, and oysters), gastropoda (snails and slugs), cephalopoda (octopus, squid, and chambered nautilus), scaphopoda, amphineura (chitons), and monoplacophora.

Annelida: This phylum includes the classes oligochaeta (earthworms), polychaeta (clam worms), and hirudinea (leeches). They have true coeloms enclosed within the mesoderm. They are segmented, have repeating units, and have a nerve trunk.

Arthropoda: The phylum is diverse and populous. Members can be found in all types of environments. They have external skeletons, jointed appendages, bilateral symmetry, and nerve cords. They also have open circulatory systems and sense organs. Subphyla include crustacea (lobster, barnacles, pill bugs, and daphnia), hexapoda (all insects, which have three body segments, six legs, and usual wings), myriapoda (centipedes and millipedes), and chelicerata (the horseshoe crab and arachnids). Pill bugs have gills. Bees, ants, and wasps belong to the order hymenoptera. Like several other insect orders, they undergo complete metamorphosis.

Animal phyla

These four animal phyla lack a coelom or have a pseudocoelom.
Porifera: These are sponges. They lack a coelom and get food as water flows through them. They are usually found in marine and sometimes in freshwater environments. They are perforated and diploblastic, meaning there are two layers of cells.
Cnidaria: Members of this phylum are hydrozoa, jellyfish, and obelia. They have radial symmetry, sac-like bodies, and a polyp or medusa (jellyfish) body plan. They are diploblastic, possessing both an ectoderm and an endoderm. Food can get in through a cavity, but members of this phylum do not have an anus.

Platyhelminthes: These are also known as flatworms. Classes include turbellaria (planarian) and trematoda (which include lung, liver, and blood fluke parasites). They have organs and bilateral symmetry. They have three layers of tissue: an ectoderm, a mesoderm, and an endoderm.

Nematoda: These are roundworms. Hookworms and many other parasites are members of this phylum. They have a pseudocoelom, which means the coelom is not completely enclosed within the mesoderm. They also have a digestive tract that runs directly from the mouth to the anus. They are nonsegmented.

Extrinsic

Extrinsic refers to homeostatic systems that are controlled from outside the body. In higher animals, the nervous system and endocrine system help regulate body functions by responding to stimuli. Hormones in animals regulate many processes, including growth, metabolism, reproduction, and fluid balance. The names of hormones tend to end in "-one." Endocrine hormones are proteins or steroids. Steroid hormones (anabolic steroids) help control the manufacture of protein in muscles and bones.

Invertebrates do not have a backbone, whereas vertebrates do. The great majority of animal species (an estimated 98 percent) are invertebrates, including worms, jellyfish, mollusks, slugs, insects, and spiders. They comprise 30 phyla in all. Vertebrates belong to the phylum chordata. The vertebrate body has two cavities. The thoracic cavity holds the heart and lungs and the abdominal cavity holds the digestive organs. Animals with exoskeletons have skeletons on the outside. Examples are crabs and turtles. Animals with endoskeletons have skeletons on the inside. Examples are humans, tigers, birds, and reptiles.

Animal deuterostomic phyla

Members of the deuterostomic phyla have anuses that are formed from blastopores.

Echinodermata: Members of this phylum have radial symmetry, are marine organisms, and have a water vascular system. Classes include echinoidea (sea urchins and sand dollars), crinoidea (sea lilies), asteroidea (starfish), ophiuroidea (brittle stars), and holothuroidea (sea cucumbers).

Chordata: This phylum includes humans and all other vertebrates, as well as a few invertebrates (urochordata and cephalochordata). Members of this phylum include agnatha (lampreys and hagfish), gnathostomata, chondrichthyes (cartilaginous fish-like sharks, skates, and rays), osteichthyes (bony fishes, including ray-finned fish that humans eat), amphibians (frogs, salamander, and newts), reptiles (lizards, snakes, crocodiles, and dinosaurs), birds, and mammals.

Animal systems and structure

Systems in animals have developed to perform various functions, including providing physical protection and obtaining food. Some animals have internal or external skeletons, shells, or skin that provide protection and support. Skin helps prevent water loss. Muscle systems enable movement. Brains and nervous systems help animals respond to external stimuli by processing incoming and outgoing signals. The main systems in animals are skeletal, muscular, nervous, digestive, respiratory, reproductive, and circulatory. The human stomach, for example, aids in the process of turning consumed food sources into energy. It has many tissue types: smooth muscle tissue, loose connective tissue, nervous tissue, blood, and columnar epithelial tissue. Many animals have a stomach or digestive chamber with two openings. These are known as metazoans.

Animal tissue types

Animals have four main tissues types: epithelial, connective, muscle, and bone. Epithelial tissue is found on body surfaces (like skin) and lining body cavities (like the stomach). Its function is to form and protect various glands. The three types of epithelial tissue are squamous (flattened), cuboidal (cube-shaped), and columnar (elongated). It can be further classified as simple (a single layer) or stratified (more than one layer). Epithelial cells move substances in, around, and out of the body. They can also have protective and secretory functions. Glands comprised of epithelial tissue can be unicellular or multicellular. Connective tissue is used to bind, support, protect, form blood, store fat, and fill space. The two kinds of connective tissue are loose and fibrous. In the human body, cartilage, bone, tendons, ligaments, blood, and protective layers on muscle, nerve, and blood vessels are types of connective tissue. The three types of muscle tissue are skeletal (striated), smooth, and cardiac.

Organ systems

The 11 major organ systems are: skeletal, muscular, nervous, digestive, respiratory, circulatory, skin, excretory, immune, endocrine, and reproductive.

Skeletal: This consists of the bones and joints. The skeletal system provides support for the body through its rigid structure, provides protection for internal organs, and works to make organisms motile. Growth hormone affects the rate of reproduction and the size of body cells, and also helps amino acids move through membranes.

Muscular: This includes the muscles. The muscular system allows the body to move and respond to its environment.

Nervous: This includes the brain, spinal cord, and nerves. The nervous system is a signaling system for intrabody communications among systems, responses to stimuli, and interaction within an environment. Signals are electrochemical. Conscious thoughts and memories and sense interpretation occur in the nervous system. It also controls involuntary muscles and functions, such as breathing and the beating of the heart.

Muscle in mammals

Skeletal muscle is strong, quick, and capable of voluntary contraction. Skeletal muscle fibers are striated and cylinder shaped. They have about 25 nuclei that are located to the side of the cell. Skeletal muscle consists of myofibrils that contain two types of filaments (myofilaments) made of proteins. The two types of filaments are actin and myosin. These filaments are aligned, giving the appearance of striation. During contraction, they slide against each other and become more overlapped. Smooth muscle is weak, slow, and usually contracts involuntarily. Examples in humans can be found in the gastrointestinal tract, blood vessels, bladder, uterus, hair follicles, and parts of the eye. Smooth muscle fibers are not striated, but spindle shaped. They are somewhat long and a little wider in the center. Each cell contains one nucleus that is centrally located. Smooth muscle cells also contain myofibrils, but they are not aligned. Cardiac muscle is strong, quick, and continuously contracts involuntarily. It is found in the myocardium of the heart.

Circulatory and skin systems

Circulatory: This includes the heart, blood, and blood vessels, such as veins, arteries, and capillaries. Blood transports oxygen and nutrients to cells and carbon dioxide to the lungs.

Skin (integumentary): This includes skin, hair, nails, sense receptors, sweat glands, and oil glands. The skin is a sense organ, provides an exterior barrier against disease, regulates body temperature through perspiration, manufactures chemicals and hormones, and provides a place for nerves from the nervous system and parts of the circulation system to travel through. Skin has three layers: epidermis, dermis, and subcutaneous. The epidermis is the thin, outermost, waterproof layer. Basal cells are located in the epidermis. The dermis contains the sweat glands, oil glands, and hair follicles. The subcutaneous layer has connective tissue, and also contains adipose (fat) tissue, nerves, arteries, and veins.

Digestive and respiratory systems

Digestive: This includes the mouth, pharynx, esophagus, stomach, intestines, rectum, anal canal, teeth, salivary glands, tongue, liver, gallbladder, pancreas, and appendix. The system helps change food into a form that the body can process and use for energy and nutrients. Food is eventually eliminated as solid waste. Digestive processes can be mechanical, such as chewing food and churning it in the stomach, and chemical, such as secreting hydrochloric acid to kill bacteria and converting protein to amino acids. The overall system converts large food particles into molecules so the body can use them. The small intestine transports the molecules to the circulatory system. The large intestine absorbs nutrients and prepares the unused portions of food for elimination.

Respiratory: This includes the nose, pharynx, larynx, trachea, bronchi, and lungs. It is involved in gas exchange, which occurs in the alveoli. Fish have gills instead of lungs.

Endocrine system

The endocrine system includes the pituitary gland, pineal gland, hypothalamus, thyroid gland, parathyroids, thymus, adrenals, pancreas, ovaries, and testes. It controls systems and processes by secreting hormones into the blood system. Exocrine glands are those that secrete fluid into ducts. Endocrine glands secrete hormones directly into the blood stream without the use of ducts. Prostaglandin (tissue hormones) diffuses only a short distance from the tissue that created it, and influences nearby cells only. Adrenal glands are located above each kidney. The cortex secretes some sex hormones, as well as mineralocorticoids and glucocorticoids involved in immune suppression and stress response. The medulla secretes epinephrine and norepinephrine. Both elevate blood sugar, increase blood pressure, and accelerate heart rate. Epinephrine also stimulates heart muscle. The islets of Langerhans are clumped within the pancreas and secrete glucagon and insulin, thereby regulating blood sugar levels. The four parathyroid glands at the rear of the thyroid secrete parathyroid hormone.

Excretory, immune, and reproductive systems

Excretory: This includes the kidneys, ureters, bladder, and urethra. The excretory system helps maintain the amount of fluids in the body. Wastes from the blood system and excess water are removed in urine. The system also helps remove solid waste.

Immune: This includes the lymphatic system, lymph nodes, lymph vessels, thymus, and spleen. Lymph fluid is moved throughout the body by lymph vessels that provide protection against disease. This system protects the body from external intrusions, such as microscopic organisms and foreign substances. It can also protect against some cancerous cells.

Reproductive: In the male, this system includes the testes, vas deferens, urethra, prostate, penis, and scrotum. In the female, this system includes the ovaries, fallopian tubes (oviduct and uterine tubes), cervix, uterus, vagina, vulva, and mammary glands. Sexual reproduction helps provide genetic diversity as gametes from each parent contribute half the DNA to the zygote offspring. The system provides a method of transporting the male gametes to the female. It also allows for the growth and development of the embryo. Hormones involved are testosterone, interstitial cell stimulating hormone (ICSH), luteinizing hormone (LH), follicle stimulating hormone (FSH), and estrogen. Estrogens secreted from the ovaries include estradiol, estrone, and estriol. They encourage growth, among other things. Progesterone helps prepare the endometrium for pregnancy.

Reproductive systems in animals

Based on whether or not and when an organism uses meiosis or mitosis, the three possible cycles of reproduction are haplontic, diplontic, and haplodiplontic. Fungi, green algae, and protozoa are haplontic. Animals and some brown algae and fungi are diplontic. Plants and some fungi are haplodiplontic. Diplontic organisms, like multicelled animals, have a dominant diploid life cycle. The haploid generation is simply the egg and sperm. Monoecious species are bisexual (hermaphroditic). In this case, the individual has both male and female organs: sperm-bearing testicles and egg-bearing ovaries. Hermaphroditic species can self fertilize. Some worms are hermaphroditic. Cross fertilization is when individuals exchange genetic information. Most animal species are dioecious, meaning individuals are distinctly male or female.

Hormones

The small cone-like pineal glands located in the brain secrete melatonin, which acts as a biological clock. The dual-lobed pituitary gland in the brain secretes growth hormone (stimulates tissue growth), thyroid stimulating hormone (signals the body to produce thyroxin), adrenocorticotropic hormone (signals the adrenal gland to produce cortisol), follicle-stimulating hormone (signals ovarian follicles to mature in females; helps regulate sperm cell production in males), luteinizing hormone (stimulates the production of estrogens and starts ovulation; stimulates production of testosterone), melanocyte-stimulating hormone (skin tone), and prolactin (stimulates milk let-down). These are all secreted by the anterior lobe. The posterior lobe secretes antidiuretic hormone and oxytocin. The thyroid in the neck secretes thyroxine, triiodothyronine, and calcitonin. These are involved with brain development, reproductive tract functions, and metabolism regulation. The thymus secretes thymosin.

Nutritional requirements

Carbohydrates are the primary source of energy as they can be easily converted to glucose. Fats (oils or lipids) are usually not very water soluble, and vitamins A, D, E, and K are fat soluble. Fats are needed to help process these vitamins and can also store energy. Fats have the highest calorie value per gram (9,000 calories). Dietary fiber, or roughage, helps the excretory system. In humans, fiber can help regulate blood sugar levels, reduce heart disease, help food pass through the digestive system, and add bulk. Dietary minerals are chemical elements that are involved with biochemical functions in the body. Proteins consist of amino acids. Proteins are broken down in the body into amino acids that are used for protein biosynthesis or fuel. Vitamins are compounds that are not made by the body, but obtained through the diet. Water is necessary to prevent dehydration since water is lost through the excretory system and perspiration.

Classifications of animals

As heterotrophs, animals can be further classified as carnivores, herbivores, omnivores, and parasites. Predation refers to a predator that feeds on another organism, which results in its death. Detritivory refers to heterotrophs that consume organic dead matter. Carnivores are animals that are meat eaters. Herbivores are plant eaters, and omnivores eat both meat and plants. A parasite's food source is its host. A parasite lives off of a host, which does not benefit from the interaction. Nutrients can be classified as carbohydrates, fats, fiber, minerals, proteins, vitamins, and water. Each supply a specific substance required for various species to survive, grow, and reproduce. A calorie is a measurement of heat energy. It can be used to represent both how much energy a food can provide and how much energy an organism needs to live.

Vitamins

Humans need dietary vitamins, which can be classified as either water soluble or fat soluble. Vitamins A, D, E, and K are fat soluble. Vitamins C and B are water soluble. Vitamin A (retinol) can be found in milk, eggs, liver, and some vegetables and fruits. It plays a role in immune system function, cell growth, and eye function.

Vitamin C (ascorbic acid) is in berries, peppers, and citrus fruits. It helps promote cell cohesiveness and healthy bones, teeth, and gums. It also improves brain function and aids in the absorption of some minerals. Other vitamins include: D (calciferol), which strengthens bones; vitamin B_2 (riboflavin), which is found in eggs; vitamin E (tocopherol); B_{12} (cyanocobalamin), which plays a role in red blood cell and nerve function; K (phylloquinone), which is found in alfalfa; B_5 (pantothenic acid); B_7 (biotin); B_6 (pyridoxine); B_3 (niacin); B_9 (folic acid); and B_1 (thiamine), which is needed to convert carbohydrates and plays a role in heart, muscle and nervous system function.

Minerals

Dietary minerals that are necessary for humans include potassium, chloride, sodium, calcium, phosphorus, magnesium, zinc, iron, manganese, copper, iodine, selenium, and molybdenum. Potassium is involved with ATP synthesis, and can be found in beans, bananas, and potatoes. Chloride, found in salt, is involved in making hydrochloric acid in the stomach. Substances like potassium and sodium are electrolytes, which mean they are conductive. Calcium is in dairy products, nuts, and green leafy vegetables. It is involved in the functions of the muscle, heart, digestive system, and bones. Magnesium is in nuts and soy beans. It is involved in ATP synthesis. Some enzymes need zinc to function. Iron is in green leafy vegetables, fish, eggs, beans, whole and enriched grains, and red meat. It is used by proteins and enzymes. Manganese and selenium are enzyme co-factors.

Early growth in humans

The zygote has genetic information from both parent organisms. After fertilization, the zygote undergoes many mitotic divisions, also called cleavage, by which the cell divides and grows into a morula and then a blastula. This hollow sphere undergoes rearrangement and differentiation. In sponges, blastula larvae swim to a new location and then form into a new individual. In humans, the blastocyst is implanted by day six or seven. It attaches to the endometrium. The blastula forms a gastrula with a digestive chamber and two germ layers: the external ectoderm and internal endoderm. In most cases, a mesoderm also develops between them. These germ layers then differentiate to form tissues and organs. Roughly two weeks after fertilization, the embryo starts to form a yolk sac that will make blood cells, an embryonic disc, and a chorion (the placenta). By week three, the beginnings of the spinal cord, brain, muscles, bones, and face appear. After that, cardiac cells begin to beat.

Changes that can lead to disease

Sometimes, the body's immune system attacks its own cells even when they are harmless. Faulty genes can lead to body parts and systems that do not function properly. Viruses, which can get introduced to the body in a variety of ways, can cause gastrointestinal pain and destroy immune system cells, which leave the body vulnerable to secondary bacterial infections and cancer cell growth. Cardiac dysfunction is a response (a compensatory mechanism) to the heart trying to maintain normal heart function. Eventually, this causes the cardiac system to weaken. When the heart muscle contracts to pump blood out, it is referred to as systolic blood flow. When the heart muscle relaxes and blood flows back in, it is referred to as diastolic blood flow. If there are problems related to systolic and/or diastolic blood flow, the amount of blood output can be lessened. The ventricle can become stiffer and will not completely fill. Dysfunction can cause the heart to try to compensate and maintain normalcy by pumping harder.

Lipid, organelle, RNA, polymer, monomer, nucleotides, and nucleoid

Lipids take many forms and have varying functions, such as storing energy and acting as a building block of cell membranes. Lipids are produced by anabolysis.

Organelle: This is a general term that refers to an organ or smaller structure within a cell. Membrane-bound organelles are found in eukaryotic cells.

RNA: RNA is short for ribonucleic acid, which is a type of molecule that consists of a long chain (polymer) of nucleotide units.

Polymer: This is a compound of large molecules formed by repeating monomers.

Monomer: A monomer is a small molecule. It is a single compound that forms chemical bonds with other monomers to make a polymer.

Nucleotides: These are molecules that combine to form DNA and RNA. They can be easily stained to make them more visible.

Nucleoid: This is the nucleus-like, irregularly-shaped mass of DNA that contains the chromatin in a prokaryotic cell.

Mitochondria functions

Four functions of mitochondria are: the production of cell energy, cell signaling (how communications are carried out within a cell, cellular differentiation (the process whereby a non-differentiated cell becomes transformed into a cell with a more specialized purpose), and cell cycle and growth regulation (the process whereby the cell gets ready to reproduce and reproduces). Mitochondria are numerous in eukaryotic cells. There may be hundreds or even thousands of mitochondria in a single cell. Mitochondria can be involved in many functions, their main one being supplying the cell with energy. Mitochondria consist of an inner and outer membrane. The inner membrane encloses the matrix, which contains the mitochondrial DNA (mtDNA) and ribosomes. Between the inner and outer membranes are folds (cristae). Chemical reactions occur here that release energy, control water levels in cells, and recycle and create proteins and fats. Aerobic respiration also occurs in the mitochondria.

Cellular respiration

Cellular respiration refers to a set of metabolic reactions that convert chemical bonds into energy stored in the form of ATP. Respiration includes many oxidation and reduction reactions that occur thanks to the electron transport system within the cell. Oxidation is a loss of electrons and reduction is a gain of electrons. Electrons in C-H (carbon/hydrogen) and C-C (carbon/carbon) bonds are donated to oxygen atoms. Processes involved in cellular respiration include glycolysis, the Krebs cycle, the electron transport chain, and chemiosmosis. The two forms of respiration are aerobic and anaerobic. Aerobic respiration is very common, and oxygen is the final electron acceptor. In anaerobic respiration, the final electron acceptor is not oxygen. Aerobic respiration results in more ATP than anaerobic respiration. Fermentation is another process by which energy is converted.

Photosynthesis

Photosynthesis is the conversion of sunlight into energy in plant cells, and also occurs in some types of bacteria and protists. Carbon dioxide and water are converted into glucose during photosynthesis, and light is required during this process. Cyanobacteria are thought to be the descendants of the first organisms to use photosynthesis about 3.5 billion years ago. Photosynthesis is a form of cellular respiration. It occurs in chloroplasts that use thylakoids, which are structures in the membrane that contain light reaction chemicals. Chlorophyll is a pigment that absorbs light. During the process, water is used and oxygen is released. The equation for the chemical reaction that occurs during photosynthesis is $6H_2O + 6CO_2 \rightarrow C_6H_{12}O_6 + 6O_2$. During photosynthesis, six molecules of water and six molecules of carbon dioxide react to form one molecule of sugar and six molecules of oxygen.

Cell transport mechanisms

Active transport mechanisms include exocytosis and endocytosis. Active transport involves transferring substances from areas of lower concentration to areas of higher concentration. Active transport requires energy in the form of ATP. Endocytosis is the ingestion of large particles into a cell, and can be categorized as phagocytosis (ingestion of a particle), pinocytosis (ingestion of a liquid), or receptor mediated. Endocytosis occurs when a substance is too large to cross a cell membrane. Endocytosis is a process by which eukaryotes ingest food particles. During phagocytosis, cell eating vesicles used during ingestion are quickly formed and unformed. Pinocytosis is also known as cell drinking. Exocytosis is the opposite of endocytosis. It is the expulsion or discharge of substances from a cell. A lysosome digests particles with enzymes, and can be expelled through exocytosis. A vacuole containing the substance to be expelled attaches to the cell membrane and expels the substance.

Passive transport mechanisms

Transport mechanisms allow for the movement of substances through membranes. Passive transport mechanisms include simple and facilitated diffusion and osmosis. They do not require energy from the cell. Diffusion is when particles are transported from areas of higher concentration to areas of lower concentration. When equilibrium is reached, diffusion stops. Examples are gas exchange (carbon dioxide and oxygen) during photosynthesis and the transport of oxygen from air to blood and from blood to tissue. Facilitated diffusion is when specific molecules are transported by a specific carrier protein. Carrier proteins vary in terms of size, shape, and charge. Glucose and amino acids are examples of substances transported by carrier proteins. Osmosis is the diffusion of water through a semi-permeable membrane from an area of higher concentration to one of lower concentration. Examples of osmosis include the absorption of water by plant roots and the alimentary canal. Plants lose and gain water through osmosis. A plant cell that swells because of water retention is said to be turgid.

Cell cycle

The term cell cycle refers to the process by which a cell reproduces, which involves cell growth, the duplication of genetic material, and cell division. Complex organisms with many cells use the cell cycle to replace cells as they lose their functionality and wear out. The entire cell cycle in animal cells can take 24 hours. The time required varies among different cell types. Human skin cells, for example, are constantly reproducing. Some other cells only divide infrequently. Once neurons are mature, they do not grow or divide. The two ways that cells can reproduce are through meiosis and mitosis. When cells replicate through mitosis, the "daughter cell" is an exact replica of the parent cell. When cells divide through meiosis, the daughter cells have different genetic coding than the parent cell. Meiosis only happens in specialized reproductive cells called gametes.

Water and gases

Water molecules are important for many reasons. Most cells are mainly composed of water, water is a great solvent for ionic compounds such as salts, water acts as a transport medium for polar solutes, metabolic reactions happen in solutions that contain water, water can act as a temperature buffer for enzyme-catalyzed reactions, water is used in photosynthesis, and water molecules are used or formed in oxidation and reduction reactions. Carbon dioxide is used by plants during photosynthesis, which produces oxygen. Oxygen is used by organisms during respiration. Nitrogen is also used by organisms. Nitrogen is a nutrient for plants, and is also used in the formation of amino and nucleic acids after it is reduced (nitrogen fixation), which is important for cell growth and reproduction. Gases are also used during the formation and break down of biologically important molecules, including proteins, nucleic acids, carbohydrates, and lipids. Carbohydrates, for example, are made of carbon, hydrogen, and oxygen.

Cell division

Cell division is performed in organisms so they can grow and replace cells that are old, worn out, or damaged.

Chromatids: During cell division, the DNA is replicated, and chromatids are the two identical replicated pieces of chromosome that are joined at the centromere to form an "X."

Gametes: These are cells used by organisms to reproduce sexually. Gametes in humans are haploid, meaning they contain only half of the organism's genetic information (23 chromosomes). Other human cells contain all 46 chromosomes.

Haploid/diploid: Haploid means there is one set of chromosomes. Diploid means there are two sets of chromosomes (one set from each parent).

Cytokinesis: This is the splitting of a cell (including the cytoplasm) into two cells. Some believe this occurs following telophase. Others say it occurs from anaphase, as the cell begins to furrow, through telophase, when the cell actually splits into two.

Homeostasis, gene expression, transcription, translation, and cellular differentiation

Homeostasis: This describes the ability and tendency of an organism, cell, or body to adjust to environmental changes to maintain equilibrium.

Gene expression: This refers to the use of information in a gene, usually during the processes of transcription and translation, that result in a protein product.

Transcription: This refers to the synthesis of RNA. Information is provided by DNA.

Translation: This is the decoding of mRNA (messenger RNA) used in the fabrication of protein. It occurs after transcription.

Cellular differentiation: This is the process by which a less specialized cell becomes a more specialized cell.

Size: The size of the nucleus in a eukaryotic cell is about 6 micrometers (μm). It occupies about 10 percent of the cell. A chloroplast is about 1 μm. Plant and animal cell sizes range from about 10 μm to 100 μm, while the sizes of bacteria range from about 1 μm to 10 μm. Atoms have a size of about 0.1 nanometers.

DNA

Chromosomes consist of genes, which are single units of genetic information. Genes are made up of deoxyribonucleic acid (DNA). DNA is a nucleic acid located in the cell nucleus. There is also DNA in the mitochondria. DNA replicates to pass on genetic information. The DNA in almost all cells is the same. It is also involved in the biosynthesis of proteins. The model or structure of DNA is described as a double helix. A helix is a curve, and a double helix is two congruent curves connected by horizontal members. The model can be likened to a spiral staircase. It is right-handed. The British scientist Rosalind Elsie Franklin is credited with taking the x-ray diffraction image in 1952 that was used by Francis Crick and James Watson to formulate the double-helix model of DNA and speculate about its important role in carrying and transferring genetic information.

DNA structure

DNA has a double helix shape, resembles a twisted ladder, and is compact. It consists of nucleotides. Nucleotides consist of a five-carbon sugar (pentose), a phosphate group, and a nitrogenous base. Two bases pair up to form the rungs of the ladder. The "side rails" or backbone consists of the covalently bonded sugar and phosphate. The bases are attached to each other with hydrogen bonds, which are easily dismantled so replication can occur. Each base is attached to a phosphate and to a sugar. There are four types of nitrogenous bases: adenine (A), guanine (G), cytosine (C), and thymine (T). There are about 3 billion bases in human DNA. The bases are mostly the same in everybody, but their order is different. It is the order of these bases that creates diversity in people. Adenine (A) pairs with thymine (T), and cytosine (C) pairs with guanine (G).

DNA replication

Pairs of chromosomes are composed of DNA, which is tightly wound to conserve space. When replication starts, it unwinds. The steps in DNA replication are controlled by enzymes. The enzyme helicase instigates the deforming of hydrogen bonds between the bases to split the two strands. The splitting starts at the A-T bases (adenine and thymine) as there are only two hydrogen bonds. The cytosine-guanine base pair has three bonds. The term "origin of replication" is used to refer to where the splitting starts. The portion of the DNA that is unwound to be replicated is called the replication fork. Each strand of DNA is transcribed by an mRNA. It copies the DNA onto itself, base by base, in a complementary manner. The exception is that uracil replaces thymine.

Types of DNA replication

Semiconservative: DNA replication is considered semiconservative because the two replicated copies of DNA each have one strand of the original parent DNA, or half of the original genetic material.

Antiparallel replication: This refers to the fact that during DNA replication, the nucleotides (A, C, G, T, and U) on leading and lagging strands run in opposite directions. RNA synthesis is said to occur in a $5' \rightarrow 3'$ (five prime to three prime) direction. That means that the phosphate group of the nucleotide that is being added to the chain, which is $5'$, is attached to the end of the chain at the end of a hydroxyl group, which is $3'$.

Base pairing: This explains how RNA transcribes DNA in an inverted fashion. C on DNA is inserted as a G on RNA, and A on DNA becomes U on RNA.

Functions of proteins in DNA replication

Many proteins are involved in the replication of DNA, and each has a specific function. Helicase is a protein that facilitates the unwinding of the double helix structure of DNA. Single strand binding (SSB) proteins attach themselves to each strand to prevent the DNA strands from joining back together. After DNA is unwound, there are leading and lagging strands. The leading strand is synthesized continuously and the lagging strand is synthesized in Okazaki fragments. Primase, an RNA polymerase (catalyzing enzyme), acts as a starting point for replication by forming short strands, or primers, of RNA. The DNA clamp, or sliding clamp, helps prevent DNA polymerase from coming apart from the strand. DNA polymerase helps form the DNA strand by linking nucleotides. As the process progresses, RNase H removes the primers. DNA ligase then links the existing shorter strands into a longer strand.

Types of RNA

RNA acts as a helper to DNA and carries out a number of other functions. Types of RNA include ribosomal RNA (rRNA), transfer RNA (tRNA), and messenger RNA (mRNA). Viruses can use RNA to carry their genetic material to DNA. Ribosomal RNA is not believed to have changed much over time. For this reason, it can be used to study relationships in organisms. Messenger RNA carries a copy of a strand of DNA and transports it from the nucleus to the cytoplasm. Transcription is the process whereby DNA uses RNA in transcription. DNA unwinds itself and serves as a template while RNA is being assembled. The DNA molecules are copied to RNA. Translation is the process whereby ribosomes use transcribed RNA to put together the needed protein. Transfer RNA is a molecule that helps in the translation process, and is found in the cytoplasm. Ribosomal RNA is in the ribosomes.

Differences between RNA and DNA

RNA and DNA differ in terms of structure and function. RNA has a different sugar than DNA. It has ribose rather than deoxyribose sugar. The RNA nitrogenous bases are adenine (A), guanine (G), cytosine (C), and uracil (U). Uracil is found only in RNA and thymine in found only in DNA. RNA consists of a single strand and DNA has two strands. If straightened out, DNA has two side rails. RNA only has one "backbone," or strand of sugar and phosphate group components. RNA uses the fully hydroxylated sugar pentose, which includes an extra oxygen compared to deoxyribose, which is the sugar used by DNA. RNA supports the functions carried out by DNA. It aids in gene expression, replication, and transportation.

Nucleotides and ester bonds

The five bases in DNA and RNA can be categorized as either pyrimidine or purine according to their structure. The pyrimidine bases include cytosine, thymine, and uracil. They are six-sided and have a single ring shape. The purine bases are adenine and guanine, which consist of two attached rings. One ring has five sides and the other has six. When combined with a sugar, any of the five bases become nucleosides. Nucleosides formed from purine bases end in "osine" and those formed from pyrimidine bases end in "idine." Adenosine and thymidine are examples of nucleosides. Bases are the most basic components, followed by nucleosides, nucleotides, and then DNA or RNA.

Ester bonds are bonds in organic compounds that are formed by alcohol and organic acids. Water is typically a product when ester bonds are formed. Fats have ester bonds formed by fatty acids and glycerol (an alcohol).

Codons

Codons are groups of three nucleotides on the messenger RNA, and can be visualized as three rungs of a ladder. A codon has the code for a single amino acid. There are 64 codons but 20 amino acids. More than one combination, or triplet, can be used to synthesize the necessary amino acids. For example, AAA (adenine-adenine-adenine) or AAG (adenine-adenine-guanine) can serve as codons for lysine. These groups of three occur in strings, and might be thought of as frames. For example, AAAUCUUCGU, if read in groups of three from the beginning, would be AAA, UCU, UCG, which are codons for lysine, serine, and serine, respectively. If the same sequence was read in groups of three starting from the second position, the groups would be AAU (asparagine), CUU (proline), and so on. The resulting amino acids would be completely different. For this reason, there are start and stop codons that indicate the beginning and ending of a sequence (or frame). AUG (methionine) is the start codon. UAA, UGA, and UAG, also known as ocher, opal, and amber, respectively, are stop codons

Mutations

Gene disorders are the result of DNA mutations. DNA mutations lead to unfavorable gene disorders, but also provide genetic variability. This diversity can lead to increased survivability of a species. Mutations can be neutral, beneficial, or harmful. Mutations can be hereditary, meaning they are passed from parent to child. Polymorphism refers to differences in humans, such as eye and hair color, that may have originally been the result of gene mutations, but are now part of the normal variation of the species. Mutations can be de novo, meaning they happen either only in sex cells or shortly after fertilization. They can also be acquired, or somatic. These are the kinds that happen as a result of DNA changes due to environmental factors or replication errors. Mosaicism is when a mutation happens in a cell during an early embryonic stage. The result is that some cells will have the mutation andsome will not.

DNA level mutation

A DNA mutation occurs when the normal gene sequence is altered. Mutations can happen when DNA is damaged as a result of environmental factors, such as chemicals, radiation, or ultraviolet rays from the sun. It can also happen when errors are made during DNA replication. The phosphate-sugar side rail of DNA can be damaged if the bonds between oxygen and phosphate groups are disassociated. Translocation happens when the broken bonds attempt to bond with other DNA. This repair can cause a mutation. The nucleotide itself can be altered. A C, for example, might look like a T. During replication, the damaged C is replicated as a T and paired with a G, which is incorrect base pairing. Another way mutations can occur is if an error is made by the DNA polymerase while replicating a base. This happens about once for every 100,000,000 bases. A repair protein proofreads the code, however, so the mistake is usually repaired.

Ribosomes and tRNA anticodons

When the DNA is unwound during transcription, the mRNA makes a complimentary copy of codons, during which T becomes A, C becomes G, etc. During translation, the rRNA interprets the code again in a complementary fashion. A becomes U (there is no T), G becomes C, etc. Ribosomes make proteins from amino acids by using the information on mRNA as a template for sequencing amino acids in a protein. Transfer RNA (tRNA) carries amino acids that have attached to it to the ribosome. The anticodons on the tRNA are a string of triplet bases that are complementary to the mRNA. For example, a codon that is AAA on the mRNA would be associated with the anticodon UUU on the tRNA. Another example is that GGG on mRNA would be associated with the anticodon CCC on tRNA.

Translocation

Translocation is a genetic mutation in which one piece of a chromosome is transferred to another chromosome. Burkitt's lymphoma, chronic myelogenous leukemia, and Down syndrome are all examples. Trisomy 21, or Down syndrome, occurs when a copy of chromosome 21 attaches to chromosome 14. Most Down syndrome cases are caused by a pair of chromosomes (the 21st) that does not split during meiosis. Both divided cells will have an abnormal number of chromosomes. One will have 22 and the other will have 24. When this egg gets fertilized, it will have three copies of chromosome 21 instead of two. Down syndrome can also be caused by translocation between the 14th and 21st chromosomes. In these instances, genetic material is swapped. There are 200 to 250 genes on the 21st chromosome. The overexpression of the gene results in the following Down syndrome traits: premature aging, decreased immune system function, heart defects, skeletal abnormalities, disruption of DNA synthesis and repair, intellectual disabilities, and cataracts.

Mendel's laws

Mendel's laws are the law of segregation (the first law) and the law of independent assortment (the second law). The law of segregation states that there are two alleles and that half of the total number of alleles are contributed by each parent organism. The law of independent assortment states that traits are passed on randomly and are not influenced by other traits. The exception to this is linked traits. A Punnett square can illustrate how alleles combine from the contributing genes to form various phenotypes. One set of a parent's genes are put in columns, while the genes from the other parent are placed in rows. The allele combinations are shown in each cell. When two different alleles are present in a pair, the dominant one is expressed. A Punnett square can be used to predict the outcome of crosses.

Gene, genotype, phenotype, and allele

A gene is a portion of DNA that identifies how traits are expressed and passed on in an organism. A gene is part of the genetic code. Collectively, all genes form the genotype of an individual. The genotype includes genes that may not be expressed, such as recessive genes. The phenotype is the physical, visual manifestation of genes. It is determined by the basic genetic information and how genes have been affected by their environment. An allele is a variation of a gene. Also known as a trait, it determines the manifestation of a gene. This manifestation results in a specific physical appearance of some facet of an organism, such as eye color or height. For example the genetic information for eye color is a gene. The gene variations responsible for blue, green, brown, or black eyes are called alleles. Locus (pl. loci) refers to the location of a gene or alleles.

Monohybrid and hybrid crosses

Genetic crosses are the possible combinations of alleles, and can be represented using Punnett squares. A monohybrid cross refers to a cross involving only one trait. Typically, the ratio is 3:1 (DD, Dd, Dd, dd), which is the ratio of dominant gene manifestation to recessive gene manifestation. This ratio occurs when both parents have a pair of dominant and recessive genes. If one parent has a pair of dominant genes (DD) and the other has a pair of recessive (dd) genes, the recessive trait can not be expressed in the next generation because the resulting crosses all have the Dd genotype. A dihybrid cross refers to one involving more than one trait, which means more combinations are possible. The ratio of genotypes for a dihybrid cross is 9:3:3:1 when the traits are not linked. The ratio for incomplete dominance is 1:2:1, which corresponds to dominant, mixed, and recessive phenotypes.

Dominant and recessive genes

Gene traits are represented in pairs with an upper case letter for the dominant trait (A) and a lower case letter for the recessive trait (a). Genes occur in pairs (AA, Aa, or aa). There is one gene on each chromosome half supplied by each parent organism. Since half the genetic material is from each parent, the offspring's traits are represented as a combination of these. A dominant trait only requires one gene of a gene pair for it to be expressed in a phenotype, whereas a recessive requires both genes in order to be manifested. For example, if the mother's genotype is Dd and the father's is dd, the possible combinations are Dd and dd. The dominant trait will be manifested if the genotype is DD or Dd. The recessive trait will be manifested if the genotype is dd. Both DD and dd are homozygous pairs. Dd is heterozygous.

Crossing over, gametes, pedigree analysis, and probability analysis

Crossing over: This refers to the swapping of genetic material between homologous chromosomes. This leads to different combinations of genes showing up in a phenotype.

This is part of gene recombination, which is when DNA breaks down and is then reassembled.

Gametes: These are the sex cells in organisms that reproduce sexually. Each gamete contains half the genetic information of the parent. They are haploid (having 23 chromosome pairs in humans). The resulting zygote, which is formed when the two gametes become one cell, is diploid (46 chromosome pairs in humans).

Pedigree analysis: This involves isolating a trait in an organism and tracing its manifestation. Pedigree charts are often used for this type of analysis. A family pedigree shows how a trait can be seen throughout generations.

Probability analysis: This calculates the chances of a particular trait or combination of traits being expressed in an organism.

Co-dominance and incomplete dominance

Co-dominance refers to the expression of both alleles so that both traits are shown. Cows, for example, can have hair colors of red, white, or red and white (not pink). In the latter color, both traits are fully expressed. The ABO human blood typing system is also co-dominant. Incomplete dominance is when both the dominant and recessive genes are expressed, resulting in a phenotype that is a mixture of the two. The fact that snapdragons can be red, white, or pink is a good example. The dominant red gene (RR) results in a red flower because of large amounts of red pigment. White (rr) occurs because both genes call for no pigment. Pink (Rr) occurs because one gene is for red and one is for no pigment. The colors blend to produce pink flowers. A cross of pink flowers (Rr) can result in red (RR), white (rr), or pink (Rr) flowers.

Non-Mendelian terms

Polygenic inheritance: This goes beyond the simplistic Mendelian concept that one gene influences one trait. It refers to traits that are influenced by more than one gene, and takes into account environmental influences on development.

Multiple alleles: Only two alleles make up a gene, but when there are three or more possible alleles, it is known as a multiple allele. A gene where only two alleles are possible is termed polymorphic.

Complete dominance: This refers the situation in which a homozygous pair of dominant alleles (AA) and a heterozygous pair of alleles (Aa) result in the same phenotype. Dominate genes have the following characteristics: they are expressed in each generation; they are passed on to roughly half the offspring; and a parent that does not express the trait can not pass it on to offspring. The Mendelian complete dominance concept states that one gene consisting of two alleles is the only factor involved in the creation of a phenotype. Most traits, however, are more complex.

Linkage

Linkage involves characteristics that are on the same chromosome. This leads to two different traits being seen together more often than not. Linkage is the exception to independent assortment. Sex-linked traits are those that occur on a sex chromosome. Autosomal refers to non-sex chromosomes. In humans, there are 22 autosomal pairs of chromosomes and a pair of sex chromosomes. Depending on the sex, pairs are either XX (female) or XY (male). Since females don't have Y chromosomes, alleles on this gene are only manifested in males. Males can only pass on sex-linked traits on the X chromosome to their daughters since sons would not receive an X from them. Hemizygous means there is only one copy of a gene. Color blindness occurs more in males than females because it is a sex-linked trait on the X chromosome. Since it is recessive, females have a better chance of expressing the dominant characteristic of non-color blindness.

ABO blood system

Human blood typing, which uses the ABO system, is an example of co-dominance and multiple alleles. Multiple alleles means there are more than two possible alleles and therefore more than just four possible gene combinations. The types of alleles are A, B, and O. A and B are co-dominant. In co-dominance, both alleles are completely expressed. A and B both produce enzymes that produce antigens. A produces type A antigens and B produces type B antigens. Antigen molecules are located on the surfaces of red blood cells. Type O does not produce enzymes, nor does it have antigens on its surface. The antigens trigger a response in the immune system to help repel foreign substances. Matching blood types during medical procedures is important since the human immune system can detect and attack blood that is a different type. Specific blood types are used in transfusions, and blood types are determined based on the proteins (or lack of proteins) contained in the blood.

Lethal allele, pleiotropy, epistasis, and karyotype

Lethal allele: This is when a mutation in an essential gene results in the death of the organism. Cystic fibrosis and Tay-Sachs disease are examples of lethal recessive alleles.

Pleiotropy: This refers to a gene that affects more than one trait.

Epistasis: This refers to the situation in which two or more genes determine a single phenotype.

Karyotype: This is a picture of genes based on a sample of blood or skin.

The non-Mendelian concept of polygenetic inheritance takes into account environmental factors on phenotypes. For example, an individual inherits genes that help determine height, but a diet lacking in certain nutrients could limit that individual's ability to reach that height. Another example is the concept of genetic disposition, which is a propensity for a certain disease that is genetically inherited, but not necessarily manifested. For example, individuals with certain skin types are more likely to develop skin cancer. If they limit their exposure to solar radiation, however, this will not necessarily occur.

Genetic engineering, cloning, restriction enzymes, and vectors

Genetic engineering: This refers to changing or manipulating an organism's genes. Other terms that may be used to refer to genetic engineering are recombinant DNA, gene splicing, cloning, and genetic modification or manipulation. Genetic engineering is different from indirect gene manipulation, in which breeding is controlled based on observable phenotypes. Genetic engineering refers to altering the genes themselves.

Cloning: There are two definitions for cloning. The first refers to the natural cloning that occurs in nature when organisms reproduce asexually and make exact copies of them. This can happen in bacteria, plants, birds, and other organisms. The definition heard more in popular culture refers to cloning as the genetic engineering of portions of DNA, cells, or entire organisms.

Blood types

There are four possible blood types: A, B, AB, and O. These types are produced by combinations of the three alleles. AA and AO lead to type A blood. BB and BO lead to type B blood. AB leads to type AB blood because the alleles are co-dominant. AB has both A protein and antigens and B protein and antigens. The O allele is recessive. OO leads to blood type O, which lacks proteins and blood-surface antigens. Blood donors with an O blood type are known as universal donors because they do not have the type of antigens that can trigger immune system responses. Blood donors with type AB blood are known as universal recipients because they do not have the antibodies that will attack A and B antigen molecules. If parents have AB and O blood, offspring have a 50% chance of having type A blood and a 0% chance of having type O blood.

Applications of genetic engineering

Diagnostic and medical applications include treating diabetes with insulin, producing human proteins, treating hemophilia, anemia, and blood clots, and manufacturing hepatitis B vaccine. Gene therapy has been used to replace defective alleles with normal alleles. For example, if a patient has a condition caused by an enzyme deficiency, replacing the defective allele enables the person to produce that enzyme. Medical forensic applications involving DNA analysis include using it to identify individuals and solve criminal cases. Agricultural applications include crop modification to develop types of wheat, cotton, and soybeans that resist weed controlling herbicides. Plants can be altered to make them grow bigger or vaccinated to make them resistant to plant viruses and insects.

Restriction enzymes: These are proteins that can recognize portions of DNA strands and cleave them at certain points.

Vectors: Vectors deliver DNA to a cell, and can include viruses and bacterial plasmids.

Recombinant DNA and gene splicing

Recombinant DNA (rDNA) refers to manipulating sequences of DNA. One portion of DNA is removed and replaced with another. Gene splicing is a way to recombine DNA. In gene splicing, base pairs of DNA are chemically cleaved. Restriction enzymes are used to perform the cutting part of gene splicing. Once base pairs are separated, different additional genetic information can be added by a vector. DNA ligase (an enzyme) is used to put the pieces back together. The process of DNA recombination happens naturally and incrementally as a result of evolution. Use of recombinant DNA produced through genetic engineering has been used in the laboratory in diagnostic, medical forensic and agricultural applications.

Human genome project

The human genome project was an international effort by scientists in 18 countries that was undertaken to gain information about human DNA. The project set out to identify all of the genes in human DNA, which number about 20,000-25,000. Other goals included: determining the sequences of the three billion base pairs comprising human DNA, inputting information collected into databases, producing tools for data analysis and making them available, and opening a discussion about the ethical, legal, and social implications of obtaining such in-depth knowledge about the genetic makeup of humans. The completed mapping and sequencing is expected to lead to further research in the fields of molecular medicine and DNA forensics. It's also expected to spur on research in related fields, such as energy source development, bioarchaeology, human migration and evolution, agriculture improvement and production, livestock breeding, and bioprocessing.

Natural selection, gradualism, and punctuated equilibrium

Natural selection: This theory developed by Darwin states that traits that help give a species a survival advantage are passed on to subsequent generations. Members of a species that do not have the advantageous trait die before they reproduce. Darwin's four principles are: from generation to generation, there are various individuals within a species; genes determine variations; more individuals are born than survive to maturation; and specific genes enable an organism to better survive.

Gradualism: This can be contrasted with punctuationism. It is the idea that evolution proceeds at a steady pace and does not include sudden developments of new species or features from one generation to the next.

Punctuated equilibrium: This can be contrasted with gradualism. It is an idea in evolutionary biology that states that evolution involves long time periods of no change (stasis) accompanied by relatively brief periods (hundreds of thousands of years) of rapid change.

Evidence supporting theory of evolution

Scientific evidence supporting the theory of evolution can be found in biogeography, comparative anatomy and embryology, the fossil record, and molecular evidence. Biogeography studies the geographical distribution of animals and plants. Evidence of evolution related to the area of biogeography includes species that are well suited for extreme environments. The fossil record shows that species lived only for a short time period before becoming extinct. The fossil record can also show the succession of plants and animals. Living fossils are existing species that have not changed much morphologically and are very similar to ancient examples in the fossil record. Examples include the horseshoe crab and ginko. Comparative embryology studies how species are similar in the embryonic stage, but become increasingly specialized and diverse as they age. Vestigial organs are those that still exist, but become nonfunctional. Examples include the hind limbs of whales and the wings of birds that can no longer fly, such as ostriches.

Rate of evolution

The rate of evolution is affected by the variability of a population. Variability increases the likelihood of evolution. Variability in a population can be increased by mutations, immigration, sexual reproduction (as opposed to asexual reproduction), and size. Natural selection, emigration, and smaller populations can lead to decreased variability. Sexual selection affects evolution. If fewer genes are available, it will limit the number of genes passed on to subsequent generations. Some animal mating behaviors are not as successful as others. A male that does not attract a female because of a weak mating call or dull feathers, for example, will not pass on its genes. Mechanical isolation, which refers to sex organs that do not fit together very well, can also decrease successful mating.

Three types of evolution

Three types of evolution are divergent, convergent, and parallel. Divergent evolution refers to two species that become different over time. This can be caused by one of the species adapting to a different environment. Convergent evolution refers to two species that start out fairly different, but evolve to share many similar traits. Parallel evolution refers to species that are not similar and do not become more or less similar over time. Mechanisms of evolution include descent (the passing on of genetic information), mutation, migration, natural selection, and genetic variation and drift. The biological definition of species refers to a group of individuals that can mate and reproduce. Speciation refers to the evolution of a new biological species. The biological species concept (BSC) basically states that a species is a community of individuals that can reproduce and have a niche in nature.

Prezygotic barriers to reproduction

Spatial: This refers to species that are separated by a distance that prevents them from mating.

Geographical: This is when species are physically separated by a barrier. A barrier can divide a population, which is known as vicariance. If a population crosses a barrier to create two species, it is known as dispersal.
Habitat: This refers to species that live in different habitats in the same area.
Temporal: This refers to the fact that species reach sexual maturity at different times. An example is plants that flower at different times of the year.

Behavioral: This refers to the fact that mating rituals distinguish interaction between sexes. For example, many species of crickets are morphologically (structurally) the same, yet a female of one species will only respond to the mating rituals of males within her species.
Mechanical: This refers to physiological structural differences that prevent mating or the transfer of gametes.

Gametic isolation: This refers to the fact that fertilization may not occur when gametes of different species are not compatible.

Allele frequency

The gene pool refers to all alleles of a gene and their combinations. The Hardy-Weinberg principle (or Castle-Hardy Weinberg principle) postulates that the allele frequency for dominant and recessive alleles will remain the same in a population through successive generations if certain conditions exist. These conditions are: no mutations, large populations, random mating, no migration, and equal genotypes. This is an ideal and not how most population's function. Changes in the frequency and types of alleles in a gene pool can be caused by gene flow, random mutation, nonrandom mating, and genetic drift. In organisms that reproduce by sexual reproduction, reproduction isolation is defined as something that acts as a barrier to two species reproducing. These barriers are classified as prezygotic and postzygotic.

Random mutations, nonrandom mating, and gene migration

Random mutations: These are genetic changes caused by DNA errors or environmental factors such as chemicals and radiation. Mutations can be beneficial or harmful.

Nonrandom mating: This refers to the fact that the probability of two individuals mating in a population is not the same for all pairs. Nonrandom mating can be caused by geographical isolation, small populations, and other factors. Nonrandom mating can lead to inbreeding (mating with a relative), which can lead to a decline in physical fitness as seen in a phenotype and the reduction of allele frequency and occurrence.

Gene migration: Also known as gene flow, gene migration is the movement of alleles to another population. This can occur through immigration, when individuals of a species move into an area, or through emigration, when individuals of a species move out of an area.

Postzygotic barriers to reproduction

Hybrid viability: This is when a hybrid zygote does not reach maturity.

Hybrid sterility: This is also known as hybrid infertility. It occurs when two species produce a hybrid offspring that reaches maturity, but is sterile. An example of this is the mule. Mules are the result of a horse and a donkey mating. Mules, however, can not reproduce.

Hybrid breakdown: This is when the first generation is not only viable, but also reaches maturity and can reproduce. Subsequent generations, however, are neither viable nor fertile.

Process of reproduction

Individuals of a species have specialized reproductive cells. These cells are responsible for meiosis, which typically results in motile spermatozoa in the male and non-motile, food-containing ova in the female (gametogenesis). Gametogenesis refers to the production of haploid gametes. Spermatogenesis refers to sperm production, which occurs in the testes. Oogenesis refers to egg formation, which takes place in the ovaries. It also produces a polar body. Before fertilization, the oocyte continues to develop in a follicle. In the female, human luteinizing hormone (LH) causes the follicle to break open and the oocyte to slowly move down the fallopian tube. Fertilization occurs when the two gametes fuse to form a zygote, which develops into an individual. Sperm needs to be deposited within five days of ovulation for fertilization to occur. The ovaries secrete estrogen and progesterone. The testes secrete testosterone. The placenta secretes chorionic gonadotropin.

Asexual reproduction

Asexual reproduction occurs when only one parent is responsible for reproduction. Forms of this include budding, fragmentation, parthenogenesis, and self-fertilization.

Budding: This occurs when the offspring start as a growth on the parent organism's body. Jellyfish and some echinoderms have buds that leave the parent. Other organisms, such as corals, continue to be attached and form colonies.

Fragmentation: This is similar to budding, but after maturity the individual fragments into about eight pieces. Each fragment develops into another mature individual. Some small worms reproduce using this method.

Parthenogenesis: This is also known as virgin birth because the female produces eggs that develop without being fertilized. Specific species of fish, insects, frogs, and lizards reproduce by parthenogenesis.

Self-fertilization: Some species are considered hermaphroditic, meaning individuals have both male and female reproductive parts. Fertilization can be achieved within the individual.

Contributing individuals to the theory of evolution

Cuvier (1744-1829)
Cuvier was a French naturalist who used the fossil record (paleontology) to compare the anatomies of extinct species and existing species to make conclusions about extinction. He believed in the catastrophism theory more strongly than the theory of evolution.

Lamarck (1769-1832)
Lamarck was a French naturalist who believed in the idea of evolution and thought it was a natural occurrence influenced by the environment. He studied medicine and botany. Lamarck put forth a theory of evolution by inheritance of acquired characteristics. He theorized that organisms became more complex by moving up a ladder of progress.

Lyell (1797-1875)
Lyell was a British geologist who believed in geographical uniformitarianism, which can be contrasted with catastrophism.

Charles Robert Darwin (1809-1882)
Darwin was an English naturalist known for his belief that evolution occurred by natural selection. He believed that species descend from common ancestors.

Alfred Russell Wallace (1823-1913)
He was a British naturalist who independently developed a theory of evolution by natural selection. He believed in the transmutation of species (that one species develops into another).

Ecosystems

Human impacts on ecosystems take many forms and have many causes. They include widespread disruptions and specific niche disturbances. Humans practice many forms of environmental manipulation that affect plants and animals in many biomes and ecosystems. Many human practices involve the consumption of natural resources for food and energy production, the changing of the environment to produce food and energy, and the intrusion on ecosystems to provide shelter. These general behaviors include a multitude of specific behaviors, including the use and overuse of pesticides, the encroachment upon habitat, over hunting and over fishing, the introduction of plant and animal species into non-native ecosystems, not recycling, and the introduction of hazardous wastes and chemical byproducts into the environment. These behaviors have led to a number of consequences, such as acid rain, ozone depletion, deforestation, urbanization, accelerated species loss, genetic abnormalities, endocrine disruption in populations, and harm to individual animals.

Social behaviors

Territoriality: This refers to members of a species protecting areas from other members of their species and from other species. Species members claim specific areas as their own.

Dominance: This refers to the species in a community that is the most populous.

Altruism: This is when a species or individual in a community exhibits behaviors that benefit another individual at a cost to itself. In biology, altruism does not have to be a conscious sacrifice.

Threat display: This refers to behavior by an organism that is intended to intimidate or frighten away members of its own or another species.

The principle of competitive exclusion (Gause's Law) states that if there are limited or insufficient resources and species are competing for them, these species will not be able to co-exist. The result is that one of the species will become extinct or be forced to undergo a behavioral or evolutionary change. Another way to say this is that "complete competitors cannot coexist."

Population

Population is a measure of how many individuals exist in a specific area. It can be used to measure the size of human, plant, or animal groups. Population growth depends on many factors. Factors that can limit the number of individuals in a population include lack of resources such as food and water, space, habitat destruction, competition, disease, and predators. Exponential growth refers to an unlimited rising growth rate. This kind of growth can be plotted on a chart in the shape of a J. Carrying capacity is the population size that can be sustained. The world's population is about 6.8 billion and growing. The human population has not yet reached its carrying capacity. Population dynamics refers to how a population changes over time and the factors that cause changes. An S-shaped curve shows that population growth has leveled off. Biotic potential refers to the maximum reproductive capacity of a population given ideal environmental conditions.

Interspecific relationships

Predation, parasitism, commensalism, and mutualism are all types of species interactions that affect species populations. Intraspecific relationships are relationships among members of a species. Interspecific relationships are relationships between members of different species.

Predation: This is a relationship in which one individual feeds on another (the prey), causing the prey to die.

Commensalism: This refers to interspecific relationships in which one of the organisms benefits. Mutualism, competition, and parasitism are all types of commensalism.

Mutualism: This is a relationship in which both organisms benefit from an interaction.

Competition: This is a relationship in which both organisms are harmed.

Parasitism: This is a relationship in which one organism benefits and the other is harmed.
Biomass: In ecology, biomass refers to the mass of one or all of the species (species biomass) in an ecosystem or area.

Community

A community is any number of species interacting within a given area. A niche is the role of a species within a community. Species diversity refers to the number of species within a community and their populations.

A biome refers to an area in which species are associated because of climate. The six major biomes in North America are desert, tropical rain forest, grassland, coniferous forest, deciduous forest, and tundra.
Biotic: Biotic factors are the living factors, such as other organisms, that affect a community or population. Abiotic factors are nonliving factors that affect a community or population, such as facets of the environment.

Ecology: Ecology is the study of plants, animals, their environments, and how they interact.

Ecosystem: An ecosystem is a community of species and all of the environment factors that affect them.

Food chains and biomagnifications

A food chain is a linking of organisms in a community that is based on how they use each other as food sources. Each link in the chain consumes the link above it and is consumed by the link below it. The exceptions are the organism at the top of the food chain and the organism at the bottom.

Biomagnification (bioamplification): This refers to an increase in concentration of a substance within a food chain. Examples are pesticides or mercury. Mercury is emitted from coal-fired power plants and gets into the water supply, where it is eaten by a fish. A larger fish eats smaller fish, and humans eat fish. The concentration of mercury in humans has now risen. Biomagnification is affected by the persistence of a chemical, whether it can be broken down and negated, food chain energetics, and whether organisms can reduce or negate the substance.

Ecoystem stability and ecologic succession

Ecosystem stability: This is a concept that states that a stable ecosystem is perfectly efficient. Seasonal changes or expected climate fluctuations are balanced by homeostasis. It also states that interspecies interactions are part of the balance of the system. Four principles of ecosystem stability are that waste disposal and nutrient replenishment by recycling is complete, the system uses sunlight as an energy source, biodiversity remains, and populations are stable in that they do not over consume resources.

Ecologic succession: This is the concept that states that there is an orderly progression of change within a community. An example of primary succession is that over hundreds of years bare rock decomposes to sand, which eventually leads to soil formation, which eventually leads to the growth of grasses and trees. Secondary succession occurs after a disturbance or major event that greatly affects a community, such as a wild fire or construction of a dam.

Biochemical cycles

Biochemical cycles are how chemical elements required by living organisms cycle between living and nonliving organisms. Elements that are frequently required are phosphorus, sulfur, oxygen, carbon, gaseous nitrogen, and water. Elements can go through gas cycles, sedimentary cycles, or both. Elements circulate through the air in a gas cycle and from land to water in a sedimentary one.

Mimicry is an adaptation developed as a response to predation. It refers to an organism that has a similar appearance to another species, which is meant to fool the predator into thinking the organism is more dangerous than it really is. Two examples are the drone fly and the io moth. The fly looks like a bee, but cannot sting. The io moth has markings on its wings that make it look like an owl. The moth can startle predators and gain time to escape. Predators can also use mimicry to lure their prey.

Food webs

A food web consists of interconnected food chains in a community. The organisms can be linked to show the direction of energy flow. Energy flow in this sense is used to refer to the actual caloric flow through a system from trophic level to trophic level. Trophic level refers to a link in a food chain or a level of nutrition. The 10% rule is that from trophic level to level, about 90% of the energy is lost (in the form of heat, for example). The lowest trophic level consists of primary producers (usually plants), then primary consumers, then secondary consumers, and finally tertiary consumers (large carnivores). The final link is decomposers, which break down the consumers at the top. Food chains usually do not contain more than six links. These links may also be referred to as ecological pyramids.

Physical Science

Physics

Thermodynamics

Thermodynamics is a branch of physics that studies the conversion of energy into work and heat. It is especially concerned with variables such as temperature, volume, and pressure. Thermodynamic equilibrium refers to objects that have the same temperature because heat is transferred between them to reach equilibrium. Thermodynamics takes places within three different types of systems; open, isolated, and closed systems. Open systems are capable of interacting with a surrounding environment and can exchange heat, work (energy), and matter outside their system boundaries. A closed system can exchange heat and work, but not matter. An isolated system cannot exchange heat, work, or matter with its surroundings. Its total energy and mass stay the same. In physics, surrounding environment refers to everything outside a thermodynamic system (system). The terms "surroundings" and "environment" are also used. The term "boundary" refers to the division between the system and its surroundings.

The laws of thermodynamics are generalized principles dealing with energy and heat.
- The zeroth law of thermodynamics states that two objects in thermodynamic equilibrium with a third object are also in equilibrium with each other. Being in thermodynamic equilibrium basically means that different objects are at the same temperature.
- The first law deals with conservation of energy. It states that neither mass nor energy can be destroyed; only converted from one form to another.
- The second law states that the entropy (the amount of energy in a system that is no longer available for work or the amount of disorder in a system) of an isolated system can only increase. The second law also states that heat is not transferred from a lower-temperature system to a higher-temperature one unless additional work is done.
- The third law of thermodynamics states that as temperature approaches absolute zero, entropy approaches a constant minimum. It also states that a system cannot be cooled to absolute zero.

Thermal contact refers to energy transferred to a body by a means other than work. A system in thermal contact with another can exchange energy with it through the process of heat transfer. Thermal contact does not necessarily involve direct physical contact. Heat is energy that can be transferred from one body or system to another without work being done. Everything tends to become less organized and less useful over time (entropy). In all energy transfers, therefore, the overall result is that the heat is spread out so that objects are in thermodynamic equilibrium and the heat can no longer be transferred without additional work.

The laws of thermodynamics state that energy can be exchanged between physical systems as heat or work, and that systems are affected by their surroundings. It can be said that the total amount of energy in the universe is constant. The first law is mainly concerned with the conservation of energy and related concepts, which include the statement that energy can only be transferred or converted, not created or destroyed. The formula used to represent the first law is $\Delta U = Q - W$, where ΔU is the change in total internal energy of a system, Q is the heat added to the system, and W is the work done by the system. Energy can be transferred by conduction, convection, radiation, mass transfer, and other processes such as collisions in chemical and nuclear reactions. As transfers occur, the matter involved becomes less ordered and less useful. This tendency towards disorder is also referred to as entropy.

The second law of thermodynamics explains how energy can be used. In particular, it states that heat will not transfer spontaneously from a cold object to a hot object. Another way to say this is that heat transfers occur from higher temperatures to lower temperatures. Also covered under this law is the concept that systems not under the influence of external forces tend to become more disordered over time. This type of disorder can be expressed in terms of entropy. Another principle covered under this law is that it is impossible to make a heat engine that can extract heat and convert it all to useful work. A thermal bottleneck occurs in machines that convert energy to heat and then use it to do work. These types of machines are less efficient than ones that are solely mechanical.

Conduction is a form of heat transfer that occurs at the molecular level. It is the result of molecular agitation that occurs within an object, body, or material while the material stays motionless. An example of this is when a frying pan is placed on a hot burner. At first, the handle is not hot. As the pan becomes hotter due to conduction, the handle eventually gets hot too. In this example, energy is being transferred down the handle toward the colder end because the higher speed particles collide with and transfer energy to the slower ones. When this happens, the original material becomes cooler and the second material becomes hotter until equilibrium is reached. Thermal conduction can also occur between two substances such as a cup of hot coffee and the colder surface it is placed on. Heat is transferred, but matter is not.

Convection refers to heat transfer that occurs through the movement or circulation of fluids (liquids or gases). Some of the fluid becomes or is hotter than the surrounding fluid, and is less dense. Heat is transferred away from the source of the heat to a cooler, denser area. Examples of convection are boiling water and the movement of warm and cold air currents in the atmosphere and the ocean. Forced convection occurs in convection ovens, where a fan helps circulate hot air.

Radiation is heat transfer that occurs through the emission of electromagnetic waves, which carry energy away from the emitting object. All objects with temperatures above absolute zero radiate heat.

Heat is energy transfer (other than direct work) from one body or system to another due to thermal contact. Everything tends to become less organized and less orderly over time (entropy). In all energy transfers, therefore, the overall result is that the energy is spread out uniformly. This transfer of heat energy from hotter to cooler objects is accomplished by conduction, radiation, or convection. Temperature is a measurement of an object's stored heat energy. More specifically, temperature is the average kinetic energy of an object's particles. When the temperature of an object increases and its atoms move faster, kinetic energy also increases. Temperature is not energy since it changes and is not conserved. Thermometers are used to measure temperature.

- 53 -

There are three main scales for measuring temperature. Celsius uses the base reference points of water freezing at 0 degrees and boiling at 100 degrees. Fahrenheit uses the base reference points of water freezing at 32 degrees and boiling at 212 degrees. Celsius and Fahrenheit are both relative temperature scales since they use water as their reference point. The Kelvin temperature scale is an absolute temperature scale. Its zero mark corresponds to absolute zero. Water's freezing and boiling points are 273.15 Kelvin and 373.15 Kelvin, respectively. Where Celsius and Fahrenheit are measured is degrees, Kelvin does not use degree terminology.

- Converting Celsius to Fahrenheit: $°F = \frac{9}{5}°C + 32$
- Converting Fahrenheit to Celsius: $°C = \frac{5}{9}(°F - 32)$
- Converting Celsius to Kelvin: $K = °C + 273.15$
- Converting Kelvin to Celsius: $°C = K - 273.15$

Heat capacity, also known as thermal mass, refers to the amount of heat energy required to raise the temperature of an object, and is measured in Joules per Kelvin or Joules per degree Celsius. The equation for relating heat energy to heat capacity is $Q = C\Delta T$, where Q is the heat energy transferred, C is the heat capacity of the body, and ΔT is the change in the object's temperature. Specific heat capacity, also known as specific heat, is the heat capacity per unit mass. Every element and compound has its own specific heat. For example, it takes different amounts of heat energy to raise the temperature of the same amounts of magnesium and lead by one degree. The equation for relating heat energy to specific heat capacity is $Q = mc\Delta T$, where m represents the mass of the object, and c represents its specific heat capacity.

Some discussions of energy consider only two types of energy: kinetic energy (the energy of motion) and potential energy (which depends on relative position or orientation). There are, however, other types of energy. Electromagnetic waves, for example, are a type of energy contained by a field. Another type of potential energy is electrical energy, which is the energy it takes to pull apart positive and negative electrical charges. Chemical energy refers to the manner in which atoms form into molecules, and this energy can be released or absorbed when molecules regroup. Solar energy comes in the form of visible light and non-visible light, such as infrared and ultraviolet rays. Sound energy refers to the energy in sound waves.

Energy is constantly changing forms and being transferred back and forth. An example of a heat to mechanical energy transformation is a steam engine, such as the type used on a steam locomotive. A heat source such as coal is used to boil water. The steam produced turns a shaft, which eventually turns the wheels. A pendulum swinging is an example of both a kinetic to potential and a potential to kinetic energy transformation. When a pendulum is moved from its center point (the point at which it is closest to the ground) to the highest point before it returns, it is an example of a kinetic to potential transformation. When it swings from its highest point toward the center, it is considered a potential to kinetic transformation. The sum of the potential and kinetic energy is known as the total mechanical energy. Stretching a rubber band gives it potential energy. That potential energy becomes kinetic energy when the rubber band is released.

Motion and Force

Mechanics is the study of matter and motion, and the topics related to matter and motion, such as force, energy, and work. Discussions of mechanics will often include the concepts of vectors and scalars. Vectors are quantities with both magnitude and direction, while scalars have only magnitude. Scalar quantities include length, area, volume, mass, density, energy, work, and power. Vector quantities include displacement, velocity, acceleration, momentum, and force.

Motion is a change in the location of an object, and is the result of an unbalanced net force acting on the object. Understanding motion requires the understanding of three basic quantities: displacement, velocity, and acceleration.

Displacement
When something moves from one place to another, it has undergone *displacement*. Displacement along a straight line is a very simple example of a vector quantity. If an object travels from position x = -5 cm to x = 5 cm, it has undergone a displacement of 10 cm. If it traverses the same path in the opposite direction, its displacement is -10 cm. A vector that spans the object's displacement in the direction of travel is known as a displacement vector.

Velocity
There are two types of velocity to consider: *average velocity* and *instantaneous velocity*. Unless an object has a constant velocity or we are explicitly given an equation for the velocity, finding the instantaneous velocity of an object requires the use of calculus. If we want to calculate the *average velocity* of an object, we need to know two things: the displacement, or the distance it has covered, and the time it took to cover this distance. The formula for average velocity is simply the distance traveled divided by the time required. In other words, the average velocity is equal to the change in position divided by the change in time. Average velocity is a vector and will always point in the same direction as the displacement vector (since time is a scalar and always positive).

Acceleration
Acceleration is the change in the velocity of an object. On most test questions, the acceleration will be a constant value. Like position and velocity, acceleration is a vector quantity and will therefore have both magnitude and direction.

Most motion can be explained by Newton's three laws of motion:

Newton's first law
An object at rest or in motion will remain at rest or in motion unless acted upon by an external force. This phenomenon is commonly referred to as inertia, the tendency of a body to remain in its present state of motion. In order for the body's state of motion to change, it must be acted on by an unbalanced force.

Newton's second law
An object's acceleration is directly proportional to the net force acting on the object, and inversely proportional to the object's mass. It is generally written in equation form $F = ma$, where F is the net force acting on a body, m is the mass of the body, and a is its acceleration. Note that since the mass is always a positive quantity, the acceleration is always in the same direction as the force.

Newton's third law

For every force, there is an equal and opposite force. When a hammer strikes a nail, the nail hits the hammer just as hard. If we consider two objects, A and B, then we may express any contact between these two bodies with the equation $F_{AB} = -F_{BA}$, where the order of the subscripts denotes which body is exerting the force. At first glance, this law might seem to forbid any movement at all since every force is being countered with an equal opposite force, but these equal opposite forces are acting on different bodies with different masses, so they will not cancel each other out.

Energy

The two types of energy most important in mechanics are potential and kinetic energy. Potential energy is the amount of energy an object has stored within itself because of its position or orientation. There are many types of potential energy, but the most common is gravitational potential energy. It is the energy that an object has because of its height (h) above the ground. It can be calculated as $PE = mgh$, where m is the object's mass and g is the acceleration of gravity. Kinetic energy is the energy of an object in motion, and is calculated as $KE = mv^2/2$, where v is the magnitude of its velocity. When an object is dropped, its potential energy is converted into kinetic energy as it falls. These two equations can be used to calculate the velocity of an object at any point in its fall.

Work

Work can be thought of as the amount of energy expended in accomplishing some goal. The simplest equation for mechanical work (W) is $W = Fd$, where F is the force exerted and d is the displacement of the object on which the force is exerted. This equation requires that the force be applied in the same direction as the displacement. If this is not the case, then the work may be calculated as $W = Fd \cos(\theta)$, where θ is the angle between the force and displacement vectors. If force and displacement have the same direction, then work is positive; if they are in opposite directions, then work is negative; and if they are perpendicular, the work done by the force is zero.

As an example, if a man pushes a block horizontally across a surface with a constant force of 10 N for a distance of 20 m, the work done by the man is 200 N-m or 200 J. If instead the block is sliding and the man tries to slow its progress by pushing against it, his work done is -200 J, since he is pushing in the direction opposite the motion. If the man pushes vertically downward on the block while it slides, his work done is zero, since his force vector is perpendicular to the displacement vector of the block.

Friction

Friction is a force that arises as a resistance to motion where two surfaces are in contact. The maximum magnitude of the frictional force (f) can be calculated as $f = F_c \mu$, where F_c is the contact force between the two objects and μ is a coefficient of friction based on the surfaces' material composition. Two types of friction are static and kinetic. To illustrate these concepts, imagine a book resting on a table. The force of its weight (W) is equal and opposite to the force of the table on the book, or the normal force (N). If we exert a small force (F) on the book, attempting to push it to one side, a frictional force (f) would arise, equal and opposite to our force. At this point, it is a *static frictional force* because the book is not moving. If we increase our force on the book, we will eventually cause it to move. At this point, the frictional force opposing us will be a *kinetic frictional force*. Generally, the kinetic frictional force is lower than static frictional force (because the frictional coefficient

- 56 -

for static friction is larger), which means that the amount of force needed to maintain the movement of the book will be less than what was needed to start it moving.

Gravitational force

Gravitational force is a universal force that causes every object to exert a force on every other object. The gravitational force between two objects can be described by the formula, $F = Gm_1m_2/r^2$, where m_1 and m_2 are the masses of two objects, r is the distance between them, and G is the gravitational constant, $G = 6.672 \times 10^{-11}$ N-m^2/kg^2. In order for this force to have a noticeable effect, one or both of the objects must be extremely large, so the equation is generally only used in problems involving planetary bodies. For problems involving objects on the earth being affected by earth's gravitational pull, the force of gravity is simply calculated as $F = mg$, where g is 9.81 m/s^2 toward the ground.

Electrical force

Electrical force is a universal force that exists between any two electrically charged objects. Opposite charges attract one another and like charges repel one another. The magnitude of the force is directly proportional to the magnitude of the charges (q)and inversely proportional to the square of the distance (r) between the two objects: $F = kq_1q_2/r^2$, where k = 9 × 10^9 N-m^2/C^2. Magnetic forces operate on a similar principle.

Buoyancy

The key determiner as to whether an object will float or sink in water is its density. The general rule is that if an object is less dense than water, it floats; if it is denser than water, it sinks. The density of an object is equal to its mass divided by its volume (d = m/v). It is important to note the difference between an object's density and a material's density. Water has a density of one gram per cubic centimeter, while steel has a density approximately eight times that. Despite having a much higher material density, an object made of steel may still float. A hollow steel sphere, for instance, will float easily because the density of the object includes the air contained within the sphere. An object may also float only in certain orientations. An ocean liner that is placed in the water upside down, for instance, may not remain afloat. An object will float only if it can displace a mass of water equal to its own mass.

Archimedes's principle states that a buoyant (upward) force on a submerged object is equal to the weight of the liquid displaced by the object. This principle of buoyancy can also be used to calculate the volume of an irregularly shaped object. The mass of the object (m) minus its apparent mass in the water (m_a) divided by the density of water (ρ_w), gives the object's volume: $V = (m-m_a)/\rho_w$.

Machines

Simple machines include the inclined plane, lever, wheel and axle, and pulley. These simple machines have no internal source of energy. More complex or compound machines can be formed from them. Simple machines provide a force known as a mechanical advantage and make it easier to accomplish a task. The inclined plane enables a force less than the object's weight to be used to push an object to a greater height. A lever enables a multiplication of force. The wheel and axle allows for movement with less resistance. Single or double pulleys allows for easier direction of force. The wedge and screw are forms of the inclined plane. A wedge turns a smaller force working over a greater distance into a larger force. The screw is similar to an incline that is wrapped around a shaft.

A certain amount of work is required to move an object. The amount cannot be reduced, but by changing the way the work is performed a mechanical advantage can be gained. A certain amount of work is required to raise an object to a given vertical height. By getting to a given height at an angle, the effort required is reduced, but the distance that must be traveled to reach a given height is increased. An example of this is walking up a hill. One may take a direct, shorter, but steeper route, or one may take a more meandering, longer route that requires less effort. Examples of wedges include doorstops, axes, plows, zippers, and can openers.

A lever consists of a bar or plank and a pivot point or fulcrum. Work is performed by the bar, which swings at the pivot point to redirect the force. There are three types of levers: first, second, and third class. Examples of a first-class lever include balances, see-saws, nail extractors, and scissors (which also use wedges). In a second-class lever the fulcrum is placed at one end of the bar and the work is performed at the other end. The weight or load to be moved is in between. The closer to the fulcrum the weight is, the easier it is to move. Force is increased, but the distance it is moved is decreased. Examples include pry bars, bottle openers, nutcrackers, and wheelbarrows. In a third-class lever the fulcrum is at one end and the positions of the weight and the location where the work is performed are reversed. Examples include fishing rods, hammers, and tweezers.

The center of a wheel and axle can be likened to a fulcrum on a rotating lever. As it turns, the wheel moves a greater distance than the axle, but with less force. Obvious examples of the wheel and axle are the wheels of a car, but this type of simple machine can also be used to exert a greater force. For instance, a person can turn the handles of a winch to exert a greater force at the turning axle to move an object. Other examples include steering wheels, wrenches, faucets, waterwheels, windmills, gears, and belts. Gears work together to change a force. The four basic types of gears are spur, rack and pinion, bevel, and worm gears. The larger gear turns slower than the smaller, but exerts a greater force. Gears at angles can be used to change the direction of forces.

A single pulley consists of a rope or line that is run around a wheel. This allows force to be directed in a downward motion to lift an object. This does not decrease the force required, just changes its direction. The load is moved the same distance as the rope pulling it. When a combination pulley is used, such as a double pulley, the weight is moved half the distance of the rope pulling it. In this way, the work effort is doubled. Pulleys are never 100% efficient because of friction. Examples of pulleys include cranes, chain hoists, block and tackles, and elevators.

An electric motor converts electric energy into mechanical energy. Energy can be provided by an AC or DC source. The power provided has many practical applications. The basic premise of a motor is that the electric current passing through a wire or coil creates a magnetic field that opposes the poles of a permanent magnet. The repelling forces between one pole of the electromagnet and the opposing pole of the fixed magnet cause the coil to move about ½ a turn. As it approaches the pole of like attraction, the coil would normally stop moving. In a motor, however, the current is reversed at this time, which reverses the poles and again forces rotation. In a DC motor, a switch or commuter can be used to reverse the charge. In an AC motor, the charge alternates on its own. The coil is attached to a shaft that is rotated, which provides the mechanical energy necessary to do work.

An electrical generator is the opposite of a motor in that it transforms magnetic force into electrical energy. Like a motor, however, it uses an electromagnetic field and a permanent magnet to achieve electromagnetic induction. Generators do not create electricity, but rather convert mechanical energy into electric energy. Smaller gas generators are used as backup or primary power sources of electricity for equipment, homes, and other small-scale applications. Larger generators may use mechanical energy from many different sources, including water, steam, wind, compressed air, or even a hand crank.

Electrical Charges

Measured in watts, electric power refers to the rate at which electrical energy is transferred by an electric circuit. It can be calculated using Joule's law: $P = V*I$, where "P" is power, "V" is the potential difference (in volts) and "I" is current (in amps). Power can be generated, transmitted, and converted into various forms of light.

A watt is the unit used to measure power. One watt is equal to one joule of energy per second. A transformer is a device that uses induction to transfer current from one circuit to another. Two wound coils act as a pair of inductors. Voltage can be modified to be transferred to another circuit (as in transmission lines) or to a load, such as an electrical device plugged into a socket.

Models that can be used to explain the flow of electric current, potential, and circuits include water, gravity, and roller coasters. For example, just as gravity is a force and a mass can have a potential for energy based on its location, so can a charge within an electrical field. Just as a force is required to move an object uphill, a force is also required to move a charge from a low to high potential. Another example is water. Water does not flow when it is level. If it is lifted to a point and then placed on a downward path, it will flow. A roller coaster car requires work to be performed to transport it to a point where it has potential energy (the top of a hill). Once there, gravity provides the force for it to flow (move) downward. If either path is broken, the flow or movement stops or is not completed.

A glass rod and a plastic rod can illustrate the concept of static electricity due to friction. Both start with no charge. A glass rod rubbed with silk produces a positive charge, while a plastic rod rubbed with fur produces a negative charge. The electron affinity of a material is a property that helps determine how easily it can be charged by friction. Materials can be sorted by their affinity for electrons into a triboelectric series. Materials with greater affinities include celluloid, sulfur, and rubber. Materials with lower affinities include glass, rabbit fur, and asbestos. In the example of a glass rod and a plastic one, the glass rod rubbed with silk acquires a positive charge because glass has a lower affinity for electrons than silk. The electrons flow to the silk, leaving the rod with fewer electrons and a positive charge. When a plastic rod is rubbed with fur, electrons flow to the rod and result in a negative charge.

The attractive force between the electrons and the nucleus is called the electric force. A positive (+) charge or a negative (-) charge creates a field of sorts in the empty space around it, which is known as an electric field. The direction of a positive charge is away from it and the direction of a negative charge is towards it. An electron within the force of the field is pulled towards a positive charge because an electron has a negative charge. A particle with a positive charge is pushed away, or repelled, by another positive charge. Like charges repel each other and opposite charges attract. Lines of force show the paths of charges. Electric force between two objects is directly proportional to the product of the charge magnitudes and inversely proportional to the square of the distance between the two objects. Electric charge is measured with the unit Coulomb (C). It is the amount of charge moved in one second by a steady current of one ampere ($1C = 1A \times 1s$).

Insulators are materials that prevent the movement of electrical charges, while conductors are materials that allow the movement of electrical charges. This is because conductive materials have free electrons that can move through the entire volume of the conductor. This allows an external charge to change the charge distribution in the material. In induction, a neutral conductive material, such as a sphere, can become charged by a positively or negatively charged object, such as a rod. The charged object is placed close to the material without touching it. This produces a force on the free electrons, which will either be attracted to or repelled by the rod, polarizing (or separating) the charge. The sphere's electrons will flow into or out of it when touched by a ground. The sphere is now charged. The charge will be opposite that of the charging rod.

Charging by conduction is similar to charging by induction, except that the material transferring the charge actually touches the material receiving the charge. A negatively or positively charged object is touched to an object with a neutral charge. Electrons will either flow into or out of the neutral object and it will become charged. Insulators cannot be used to conduct charges. Charging by conduction can also be called charging by contact. The law of conservation of charge states that the total number of units before and after a charging process remains the same. No electrons have been created. They have just been moved around. The removal of a charge on an object by conduction is called grounding.

Circuits

Electric potential, or electrostatic potential or voltage, is an expression of potential energy per unit of charge. It is measured in volts (V) as a scalar quantity. The formula used is $V = E/Q$, where V is voltage, E is electrical potential energy, and Q is the charge. Voltage is typically discussed in the context of electric potential difference between two points in a circuit. Voltage can also be thought of as a measure of the rate at which energy is drawn from a source in order to produce a flow of electric charge.

A circuit is a closed path along which electrons can travel with minimal resistance except at particular locations. Electric current is the sustained flow of electrons that are part of an electric charge moving along a path in a circuit. This differs from a static electric charge, which is a constant non-moving charge rather than a continuous flow. The rate of flow of electric charge is expressed using the ampere (amp or A) and can be measured using an ammeter. A current of 1 ampere means that 1 coulomb of charge passes through a given area every second. Electric charges typically only move from areas of high electric potential to areas of low electric potential. To get charges to flow into a high potential area, you must to connect it to an area of higher potential, by introducing a battery or other voltage source.

Electric currents experience resistance as they travel through a circuit. Different objects have different levels of resistance. The ohm (Ω) is the measurement unit of electric resistance. The symbol is the Greek letter omega. Ohm's Law, which is expressed as $I = V/R$, states that current flow (I, measured in amps) through an object is equal to the potential difference from one side to the other (V, measured in volts) divided by resistance (R, measured in ohms). An object with a higher resistance will have a lower current flow through it given the same potential difference.

Movement of electric charge along a path between areas of high electric potential and low electric potential, with a resistor or load device between them, is the definition of a simple circuit. It is a closed conducting path between the high and low potential points, such as the positive and negative terminals on a battery. One example of a circuit is the flow from one terminal of a car battery to the other. The electrolyte solution of water and sulfuric acid provides work in chemical form to start the flow. A frequently used classroom example of circuits involves using a D cell (1.5 V) battery, a small light bulb, and a piece of copper wire to create a circuit to light the bulb.

Series circuits are circuits in which there is only one path through which electrons can flow. If a load in this type of circuit is removed, disabled, or switched off, the circuit is open and electricity does not flow. A parallel circuit is one in which there is more than one path through which electrons can travel. In a series circuit, the same current flows through all components. In a parallel circuit, on the other hand, the same voltage exists across all parallel paths, though the current may be vastly different among them. An example of a series circuit is a string of old-fashioned Christmas tree lights. If one bulb breaks or comes loose, the entire string will not work.

Electricity concepts and devices

Direct current (DC) is the flow of an electric charge in one direction. Batteries and solar cells typically use direct current.

Alternating current (AC) is current that periodically reverses direction. AC is typically used in houses and other buildings.

A diode is an electronic device used to conduct electric current in one direction. The process of conduction in one direction is known as rectification. A rectifier is used to convert alternating current to direct current. Diodes are also used to remove modulation from radio signals.

An inverter is the opposite of a rectifier in that it converts direct current to alternating current.
Electromotive force (emf) is what causes electrons to move when there is potential difference between two points (voltage). Devices that can provide emf include batteries, voltaic cells, thermoelectric devices, solar cells, electrical generators, transformers, and Van de Graaff generators.

Transistor is a device made of a semiconductive material that can amplify or switch an electric charge.

Semiconductor is a material with conductivity between an insulator and a conductor. These materials replaced earlier electric devices such as vacuum tubes.

Used in modern circuits, solid state devices are solid materials in which the charge carriers, or electrons, are contained entirely within the material. Examples include transistors, microprocessors, integrated circuits, light-emitting diodes (LEDs), and liquid-crystal displays (LCDs).

Magnets

A magnet is a piece of metal, such as iron, steel, or magnetite (lodestone) that can affect another substance within its field of force that has like characteristics. Magnets can either attract or repel other substances. Magnets have two poles: north and south. Like poles repel and opposite poles (pairs of north and south) attract. The magnetic field is a set of invisible lines representing the paths of attraction and repulsion. Magnetism can occur naturally, or ferromagnetic materials can be magnetized. Certain matter that is magnetized can retain its magnetic properties indefinitely and become a permanent magnet. Other matter can lose its magnetic properties. For example, an iron nail can be temporarily magnetized by stroking it repeatedly in the same direction using one pole of another magnet. Once magnetized, it can attract or repel other magnetically inclined materials, such as paper clips. Dropping the nail repeatedly will cause it to lose its charge.

The motions of subatomic structures (nuclei and electrons) produce a magnetic field. It is the direction of the spin and orbit that indicate the direction of the field. The strength of a magnetic field is known as the magnetic moment. As electrons spin and orbit a nucleus, they produce a magnetic field. Pairs of electrons that spin and orbit in opposite directions cancel each other out, creating a net magnetic field of zero. Materials that have an unpaired electron are magnetic. Those with a weak attractive force are referred to as paramagnetic materials, while ferromagnetic materials have a strong attractive force. A diamagnetic material has electrons that are paired, and therefore does not typically have a magnetic moment. There are, however, some diamagnetic materials that have a weak magnetic field.

A magnetic field can be formed not only by a magnetic material, but also by electric current flowing through a wire. When a coiled wire is attached to the two ends of a battery, for example, an electromagnet can be formed by inserting a ferromagnetic material such as an iron bar within the coil. When electric current flows through the wire, the bar becomes a magnet. If there is no current, the magnetism is lost. A magnetic domain occurs when the magnetic fields of atoms are grouped and aligned. These groups form what can be thought of as miniature magnets within a material. This is what happens when an object like an iron nail is temporarily magnetized. Prior to magnetization, the organization of atoms and their various polarities are somewhat random with respect to where the north and south poles are pointing. After magnetization, a significant percentage of the poles are lined up in one direction, which is what causes the magnetic force exerted by the material.

Waves

Waves are divided into types based on the direction of particle motion in a medium and the direction of wave propagation. Longitudinal waves are waves that travel in the same direction as the particle movement. They are sometimes called pressure, compressional, or density waves. Longitudinal sound waves are the easiest to produce and have the highest speed. A longitudinal wave consists of compressions and rarefactions, such as those seen by extending and collapsing a Slinky toy.

Shear or transverse waves waves move perpendicular to the direction of the particle movement. For example, if the particles in a medium move up and down, a transverse wave will move forward. Transverse waves are possible only in solids and are slower than longitudinal waves.Surface (circular) waves travel at the surface of a material and move in elliptical orbits. They are a little slower than shear waves. Plate waves move in elliptical orbits and only occur in very thin pieces of material.

Waves can be in phase or out of phase, which is similar to the concept of being in sync or out of sync. For example, if two separate waves originate from the same point and the peaks (crests) and valleys (troughs) are exactly aligned, they are said to be in phase. If the peak of a wave aligns with the valley of another wave, they are out of phase. When waves are in phase their displacement is doubled. If they are out of phase they cancel each other out. If they are somewhere in between being completely in phase and completely out of phase, the wave interaction is a wave that is the sum of the amplitudes of all points along the wave. If waves originate from different points, the amplitude of particle displacement is the combined sum of the particle displacement amplitude of each individual wave.

When waves traveling in the same medium interact, it is known as wave interference. While a single wave generally remains the same in terms of waveform, frequency, amplitude, and wavelength, several waves traveling through particles in a medium take on a more complicated appearance after they interact. The final properties of a wave are dependent on many factors, such as the points of origin of waves and whether they are in phase, out of phase, or somewhere in between. Constructive interference refers to what happens when two crests or two troughs of a wave meet. The resulting amplitude of the crest or trough is doubled. Destructive interference is what happens when the crest of one wave and the trough of another that are the same shape meet. When this occurs, the two waves cancel each other out. An example of destructive interference is when two unlike sound waves reduce the volume of the sound.

Waves have energy and can transfer energy when they interact with matter. Although waves transfer energy, they do not transport matter. They are a disturbance of matter that transfers energy from one particle to an adjacent particle. There are many types of waves, including sound, seismic, water, light, micro, and radio waves. The two basic categories of waves are mechanical and electromagnetic. Mechanical waves are those that transmit energy through matter. Electromagnetic waves can transmit energy through a vacuum. A transverse wave provides a good illustration of the features of a wave, which include crests, troughs, amplitude, and wavelength.

There are a number of important attributes of waves. Frequency is a measure of how often particles in a medium vibrate when a wave passes through the medium with respect to a certain point or node. Usually measured in Hertz (Hz), frequency might refer to cycles per second, vibrations per second, or waves per second. One Hz is equal to one cycle per second.

Period is a measure of how long it takes to complete a cycle. It is the inverse of frequency; where frequency is measure in cycles per second, period can be thought of as seconds per cycle, though it is measured in units of time only.

Speed refers to how fast or slow a wave travels. It is measured in terms of distance divided by time. While frequency is measured in terms of cycles per second, speed might be measured in terms of meters per second.

Amplitude is the maximum amount of displacement of a particle in a medium from its rest position, and corresponds to the amount of energy carried by the wave. High-energy waves have greater amplitudes; low energy waves have lesser amplitudes. Amplitude is a measure of a wave's strength.

Rest position, also called equilibrium, is the point at which there is neither positive nor negative displacement. Crest, also called the peak, is the point at which a wave's positive or upward displacement from the rest position is at its maximum. Trough, also called a valley, is the point at which a wave's negative or downward displacement from the rest position is at its maximum. A wavelength is one complete wave cycle. It could be measured from crest to crest, trough to trough, rest position to rest position, or any point of a wave to the corresponding point on the next wave.

Sound is a pressure disturbance that moves through a medium in the form of mechanical waves, which transfer energy from one particle to the next. Sound requires a medium to travel through, such as air, water, or other matter since it is the vibrations that transfer energy to adjacent particles, not the actual movement of particles over a great distance. Sound is transferred through the movement of atomic particles, which can be atoms or molecules. Waves of sound energy move outward in all directions from the source. Sound waves consist of compressions (particles are forced together) and rarefactions (particles move farther apart and their density decreases). A wavelength consists of one compression and one rarefaction. Different sounds have different wavelengths. Sound is a form of kinetic energy.

Pitch is the quality of sound determined by frequency. For example, a musical note can be tuned to a specific frequency. A, for instance, has a frequency of 440 Hz, which is a higher frequency than middle C. Humans can detect frequencies between about 20 Hz to 20,000 Hz.

Loudness is a human's perception of sound intensity. Sound intensity is measured as the sound power per unit area, and can be expressed in decibels.

Timbre is a human's perception of the type or quality of sound. Oscillation is a measurement, usually of time, against a basic value, equilibrium, or rest point.

The Doppler effect refers to the effect the relative motion of the source of the wave and the location of the observer has on waves. The Doppler effect is easily observable in sound waves. What a person hears when a train approaches or a car honking its horn passes by are examples of the Doppler effect. The pitch of the sound is different not because the emitted frequency has changed, but because the received frequency has changed. The frequency is higher (as is the pitch) as the train approaches, the same as emitted just as it passes, and lower as the train moves away. This is because the wavelength changes. The Doppler effect can occur when an observer is stationary, and can also occur when two trains approach and pass each other. Electromagnetic waves are also affected in this manner. The motion of the medium can also affect the wave. For waves that do not travel in a medium, such as light waves, it is the difference in velocity that determines the outcome.

The electromagnetic spectrum is defined by frequency (f) and wavelength (λ). Frequency is typically measured in hertz and wavelength is usually measured in meters. Because light travels at a fairly constant speed, frequency is inversely proportional to wavelength, a relationship expressed by the formula $f = c/\lambda$, where c is the speed of light (about 300 million meters per second). Frequency multiplied by wavelength equals the speed of the wave; for electromagnetic waves, this is the speed of light, with some variance for the medium in which it is traveling. Electromagnetic waves include (from largest to smallest wavelength) radio waves, microwaves, infrared radiation (radiant heat), visible light, ultraviolet radiation, x-rays, and gamma rays. The energy of electromagnetic waves is carried in packets that have a magnitude inversely proportional to the wavelength. Radio waves have a range of wavelengths, from about 10^{-3} to 10^5 meters, while their frequencies range from 10^3 to about 10^{11} Hz.

Atoms and molecules can gain or lose energy only in particular, discrete amounts. Therefore, they can absorb and emit light only at wavelengths that correspond to these amounts. Using a process known as spectroscopy, these characteristic wavelengths can be used to identify substances.

Light is the portion of the electromagnetic spectrum that is visible because of its ability to stimulate the retina. It is absorbed and emitted by electrons, atoms, and molecules that move from one energy level to another. Visible light interacts with matter through molecular electron excitation (which occurs in the human retina) and through plasma oscillations (which occur in metals). Visible light is between ultraviolet and infrared light on the spectrum. The wavelengths of visible light cover a range from 380 nm (violet) to 760 nm (red). Different wavelengths correspond to different colors.

The human brain interprets or perceives visible light, which is emitted from the sun and other stars, as color. For example, when the entire wavelength reaches the retina, the brain perceives the color white. When no part of the wavelength reaches the retina, the brain perceives the color black. The particular color of an object depends upon what is absorbed and what is transmitted or reflected. For example, a leaf consists of chlorophyll molecules, the atoms of which absorb all wavelengths of the visible light spectrum except for green, which is why a leaf appears green. Certain wavelengths of visible light can be absorbed when they interact with matter. Wavelengths that are not absorbed can be transmitted by transparent materials or reflected by opaque materials.

When light waves encounter an object, they are either reflected, transmitted, or absorbed. If the light is reflected from the surface of the object, the angle at which it contacts the surface will be the same as the angle at which it leaves, on the other side of the perpendicular. If the ray of light is perpendicular to the surface, it will be reflected back in the direction from which it came. When light is transmitted through the object, its direction may be altered upon entering the object. This is known as refraction. When light waves are refracted, or bent, an image can appear distorted. The degree to which the light is refracted depends on the speed at which light travels in the object. Light that is neither reflected nor transmitted will be absorbed by the surface and stored as heat energy. Nearly all instances of light hitting an object will involve a combination of two or even all three of these.

Diffraction refers to the bending of waves around small objects and the spreading out of waves past small openings. The narrower the opening, the greater the level of diffraction will be. Larger wavelengths also increase diffraction. A diffraction grating can be created by placing a number of slits close together, and is used more frequently than a prism to separate light. Different wavelengths are diffracted at different angles.

The various properties of light have numerous real life applications. For example, polarized sunglasses have lenses that help reduce glare, while non-polarized sunglasses reduce the total amount of light that reaches the eyes. Polarized lenses consist of a chemical film of molecules aligned in parallel. This allows the lenses to block wavelengths of light that are intense, horizontal, and reflected from smooth, flat surfaces. The "fiber" in fiber optics refers to a tube or pipe that channels light. Because of the composition of the fiber, light can be transmitted greater distances before losing the signal. The fiber consists of a core, cladding, and a coating. Fibers are bundled, allowing for the transmission of large amounts of data.

Geometric optics uses the concept of rays to determine how light will propagate. Ray diagrams can illustrate the path of light through a lens. Different types of lenses refract light, either convergently or divergently, to form images. After passing through a lens, rays converge at a focal point. Collimated rays are nearly parallel, and can be thought of as having no focal point. There are many types and combinations of lenses. Convergent lenses, also called positive lenses, are thicker in the middle and thinner at the edges. Rays are focused to a point. Divergent lenses, also called negative lenses, are thicker at the ends and thinner in the middle. Rays are spread apart, or diverged. A convex lens is bowed outward, either at one vertical surface or both. A convex lens with two convex surfaces may also be termed biconvex or double convex. A concave lens is bowed inward, while a planar lens is flat.

Earth Systems and the Universe

Earth's structure

The Earth is ellipsoid, not perfectly spherical. This means the diameter is different through the poles and at the equator. Through the poles, the Earth is about 12,715 km in diameter. The approximate center of the Earth is at a depth of 6,378 km. The Earth is divided into a crust, mantle, and core. The core consists of a solid inner portion. Moving outward, the molten outer core occupies the space from about a depth of 5,150 km to a depth of 2,890 km. The mantle consists of a lower and upper layer. The lower layer includes the D' (D prime) and D" (D double-prime) layers. The solid portion of the upper mantle and crust together form the lithosphere, or rocky sphere. Below this, but still within the mantle, is the asthenosphere, or weak sphere. These layers are distinguishable because the lithosphere is relatively rigid, while the asthenosphere resembles a thick liquid.

Earth's chemical composition

The Earth's core consists of hot iron and forms of nickel. The mantle consists of different materials, including iron, magnesium, and calcium. The crust covers the mantle, consists of a thin layer of much lighter rocks, and is further subdivided into continental and oceanic portions. The continental portion consists mainly of silicates, such as granite. The oceanic portion consists of heavier, volcanic rocks, such as basalt. The upper 10 miles of the lithosphere layer (the crust and part of the mantle) is made up of 95% igneous rock (or its metamorphic equivalent), 4% shale, 0.75% sandstone, and 0.25% limestone. There are over 4,000 known minerals, but only about 20 make up some 95% of all rocks. There are, however, more than 3,000 individual kinds of minerals in the Earth's crust. Silicates are the largest group of minerals.

Mountains

Orogeny refers to the formation of mountains, particularly the processes of folding and faulting caused by plate tectonics. Folding is when layers of sedimentary rock are pressed together by continental plate movements. Sections of rock that are folded upward are called anticlines. Sections of rock that are folded downward are called synclines. Examples of folded mountains are the Alps and the Himalayans. Fault-block mountains are created when tectonic plate movement produces tension that results in displacement. Mountains in the Southwest United States are examples of fault-blocking mountains. Mountains can also be caused by volcanic activity and erosion.

Tectonic Convection

Heat is transferred through the process of convection, which is a cycle. Hot material rises and spreads, cooling as it spreads. The cool material then sinks, where it is heated again. The process of convection can be seen in a pot of boiling water. It is believed this same process is happening deep within the Earth. Greater depths are associated with more pressure and heat. The weight of all the rocks causes the increase in pressure, while the decay of heavy radioactive elements such as uranium produces heat. This creates hot areas of molten material that find their way upward and to the surface in an effort to equalize, which means pressure and temperature are reduced. This causes the processes involved in plate tectonics.

Plate tectonic theory

The theory of plate tectonics states that the lithosphere, the solid portion of the mantle and Earth's crust, consists of major and minor plates. These plates are on top of and move with the viscous upper mantle, which is heated because of the convection cycle that occurs in the interior of the Earth. There are different estimates as to the exact number of major and minor plates. The number of major plates is believed to be between 9 and 15, and it is thought that there may be as many as 40 minor plates. The United States is atop the North American plate. The Pacific Ocean is atop the Pacific plate. The point at which these two plates slide horizontally along the San Andreas fault is an example of a transform plate boundary. The other two types of boundaries are divergent (plates that are spreading apart and forming new crust) and convergent (the process of subduction causes one plate to go under another). The movement of plates is what causes other features of the Earth's crust, such as mountains, volcanoes, and earthquakes.

Volcanic activities and plate tectonics

Volcanoes can occur along any type of tectonic plate boundary. At a divergent boundary, as plates move apart, magma rises to the surface, cools, and forms a ridge. An example of this is the mid-Atlantic ridge. Convergent boundaries, where one plate slides under another, are often areas with a lot of volcanic activity. The subduction process creates magma. When it rises to the surface, volcanoes can be created. Volcanoes can also be created in the middle of a plate over hot spots. Hot spots are locations where narrow plumes of magma rise through the mantle in a fixed place over a long period of time. The Hawaiian Islands and Midway are examples. The plate shifts and the island moves. Magma continues to rise through the mantle, however, which produces another island. Volcanoes can be active, dormant, or extinct. Active volcanoes are those that are erupting or about to erupt. Dormant volcanoes are those that might erupt in the future and still have internal volcanic activity. Extinct volcanoes are those that will not erupt.

Types of volcanoes

The three types of volcanoes are shield, cinder cone, and composite. A shield volcano is created by a long-term, relatively gentle eruption. This type of volcanic mountain is created by each progressive lava flow that occurs over time. A cinder cone volcano is created by explosive eruptions. Lava is spewed out of a vent into the air. As it falls to the ground, the lava cools into cinders and ash, which build up around the volcano in a cone shape. A composite volcano is a combination of the other two types of volcanoes. In this type, there are layers of lava flows and layers of ash and cinder.

Seismic deformation and seismic waves

There are two types of deformations created by an earthquake fault rupture: static and dynamic. Static deformation permanently displaces the ground. Examples are when a road or railroad track becomes distorted by an earthquake. Plate tectonics stresses the fault by creating tension with slow plate movements. An earthquake releases the tension. Plate tectonics also cause a second type of deformation. This type results in dynamic motions that

- 68 -

take the form of seismic waves. These sound waves can be compressional waves, also known as primary or P waves, or shear waves, also known as secondary or S waves. P waves travel fastest, with speeds ranging between 1.5 and 8 kilometers per second. Shear waves are slower. P waves shake the ground in the direction they are propagating. S waves shake perpendicularly or transverse to the direction of propagation. Seismographs use a simple pendulum to record earthquake movement in a record called a seismogram. A seismogram can help seismologists estimate the distance, direction, Richter magnitude, and type of faulting of an earthquake.

Earthquakes plate tectonics

Most earthquakes are caused by tectonic plate movement. They occur along fractures called faults or fault zones. Friction in the faults prevents smooth movement. Tension builds up over time, and the release of that tension results in earthquakes. Faults are grouped based on the type of slippage that occurs. The types of faults are dip-slip, strike-slip, and oblique-slip. A dip-slip fault involves vertical movement along the fault plane. In a normal dip-slip fault, the wall that is above the fault plane moves down. In a reverse dip-slip fault, the wall above the fault plane moves up. A strike-slip fault involves horizontal movement along the fault plane. Oblique-slip faults involve both vertical and horizontal movement. The Richter magnitude scale measures how much seismic energy was released by an earthquake.

Erosion

Erosion is the wearing away of rock materials from the Earth's surface. Erosion can be classified as natural geologic erosion and erosion due to human activity. Natural geologic erosion occurs due to weathering and gravity. Factors involved in natural geologic erosion are typically long term forces. Human activity such as development, farming, and deforestation occurs over shorter periods of time. Soil, which supports plant growth, is the topmost layer of organic material. One type of erosion is sheet erosion, which is the gradual and somewhat uniform removal of surface soil. Rills are small rivulets that cut into soil. Gullies are rills that have become enlarged due to extended water run-off. Sandblows are caused by wind blowing away particles. Negative effects of erosion include sedimentation in rivers, which can pollute water and damage ecosystems. Erosion can also result in the removal of topsoil, which destroys crops and prevents plants from growing. This reduces food production and alters ecosystems.

Hydrologic cycle

The hydrologic, or water, cycle refers to water movement on, above, and in the Earth. Water can be in any one of its three states during different phases of the cycle. The three states of water are liquid water, frozen ice, and water vapor. Processes involved in the hydrologic cycle include precipitation, canopy interception, snow melt, runoff, infiltration, subsurface flow, evaporation, sublimation, advection, condensation, and transpiration. Precipitation is when condensed water vapor falls to Earth. Examples include rain, fog drip, and various forms of snow, hail, and sleet. Canopy interception is when precipitation lands on plant foliage instead of falling to the ground and evaporating. Snow melt is runoff produced by melting snow. Infiltration occurs when water flows from the surface into the ground. Subsurface flow refers to water that flows underground. Evaporation is when water in a liquid state changes to a gas. Sublimation is when water in a solid state (such as snow or ice) changes to water vapor without going through a liquid phase. Advection is the movement of water through the atmosphere. Condensation is when water vapor changes to liquid water. Transpiration is when water vapor is released from plants into the air.

Deposition

Deposition, or sedimentation, is the geological process in which previously eroded material is transported or added to a land form or land mass. Erosion and sedimentation are complementary geological processes. Running water causes a substantial amount of deposition of transported materials in both fresh water and coastal areas. Examples include gravity transporting material down the slope of a mountain and depositing it at the base of the slope. Another example is when sandstorms deposit particles in other locations. When glaciers melt and retreat, it can result in the deposition of sediments. Evaporation is also considered to cause deposition since dissolved materials are left behind when water evaporates. Deposition can include the build up of organic materials. For example, chalk is partially made up of the small calcium carbonate skeletons of marine plankton, which helps create more calcium carbonate from chemical processes.

Weathering

There are two basic types of weathering: mechanical and chemical. Weathering is a very prominent process on the Earth's surface. Materials weather at different rates, which are known as differential weathering. Mechanical and chemical weathering is interdependent. For example, chemical weathering can loosen the bonds between molecules and allow mechanical weathering to take place. Mechanical weathering can expose the surfaces of land masses and allow chemical weathering to take place. Impact, abrasion, frost wedging, root wedging, salt wedging, and uploading are types of mechanical weathering. Types of chemical weathering are dissolution, hydration, hydrolysis, oxidation, biological, and carbonation. The primary type of chemical weathering is caused by water dissolving a mineral. The more acidic water is, the more effective it is at weathering. Carbonic and sulfuric acids can enter rain when they are present in the atmosphere. This lowers the pH value of rain, making it more acidic. Normal rain water has a pH value of 5.5. Acid rain has a pH value of 4 or less.

Radioactive dating

Radioactive dating, also known as radiometric dating, is a technique that can be used to determine the age of rocks and even the Earth itself. The process compares the amount of radioactive material in a rock to the amount of material that has "decayed." Decay refers to the fact that the nuclide of an element loses subatomic particles over time. The process includes a parent element that undergoes changes to create a daughter element, also known as the decay product. The daughter element can also be unstable and lose particles, creating another daughter element. This is known as a decay chain. Decay occurs until all the elements are stable. Three types of dating techniques are radiocarbon dating, potassium-argon dating, and uranium-lead dating. These techniques can be used to date a variety of natural and manmade materials, including archaeological artifacts.

Rocks and minerals

The physical properties (as opposed to chemical structures) used to identify minerals are hardness, luster, color, cleavage, streak, form (the external shape), and other special properties. Senses other than sight, such as touch, taste, and smell, may be used to observe physical properties. Hardness is the resistance a mineral has to scratches. The Mohs Hardness Scale is used to rate hardness from 1 to 10. Color can often not be determined definitively as some minerals can be more than one color. Luster is determined by reflected light. Luster can be described as metallic (shiny), sub-metallic (dull), non-metallic (vitreous, like glass), or earthy (like dirt or powder). Streak is the true color of the mineral in powdered form. It can be determined by rubbing the specimen across an unglazed porcelain tile. Fracture or cleavage is how a mineral reacts to stress, such as being struck with a hammer. Other properties that can be used to identify rocks and minerals include magnetism, a salty taste, or a pungent odor in a streak test.

Minerals are naturally occurring, inorganic solids with a definite chemical composition and an orderly internal crystal structure. A polymorph is two minerals with the same chemical composition, but a different crystal structure. Rocks are aggregates of one or more minerals, and may also contain mineraloids (minerals lacking a crystalline structure) and organic remains. The three types of rocks are sedimentary, igneous, and metamorphic. Rocks are classified based on their formation and the minerals they contain. Minerals are classified by their chemical composition. Geology is the study of the planet Earth as it pertains to the composition, structure, and origin of its rocks. Petrology is the study of rocks, including their composition, texture, structure, occurrence, mode of formation, and history. Mineralogy is the study of minerals.

Sedimentary rock

Sedimentary rocks are formed by the process of lithification, which involves compaction, the expulsion of liquids from pores, and the cementation of the pre-existing rock. It is pressure and temperature that are responsible for this process. Sedimentary rocks are often formed in layers in the presence of water, and may contain organic remains, such as fossils. Sedimentary rocks are organized into three groups: detrital, biogenic, and chemical. Texture refers to the size, shape, and grains of sedimentary rock. Texture can be used to determine how a particular sedimentary rock was created. Composition refers to the types of minerals present in the rock. The origin of sedimentary rock refers to the type of water that was involved in its creation. Marine deposits, for example, likely involved ocean environments, while continental deposits likely involved dry land and lakes.

Mineral classification

Minerals are classified by chemical composition and internal crystalline structure. They are organized into classes. Native elements such as gold and silver are not classified in this manner. The eight classes are sulfides, oxides\hydroxides, halides, carbonates, sulfates, phosphates, and silicates. These classes are based on the dominant anion (negatively charged ion) or anionic group. Minerals are classified in this way for three main reasons. First, minerals with the same anion have unmistakable resemblances. Second, minerals with the same anion are often found in the same geologic environment. For example, calcite and dolomite, which belong to the same group, are often found together. Last, this method is similar to the naming convention used to identify inorganic compounds in chemistry. Minerals can be further separated into groups on the basis of internal structure.

Metamorphic rock

Metamorphic rock is that which has been changed by great heat and pressure. This results in a variety of outcomes, including deformation, compaction, destruction of the characteristics of the original rock, bending, folding, and formation of new minerals because of chemical reactions, and changes in the size and shape of the mineral grain. For example, the igneous rock ferromagnesian can be changed into schist and gneiss. The sedimentary rock carbonaceous can be changed into marble. The texture of metamorphic rocks can be classified as foliated and unfoliated. Foliation, or layering, occurs when rock is compressed along one axis during recrystallization. This can be seen in schist and shale. Unfoliated rock does not include this banding. Rocks that are compressed equally from all sides or lack specific minerals will be unfoliated. An example is marble.

Igneous rock

Igneous rock is formed from magma, which is molten material originating from beneath the Earth's surface. Depending upon where magma cools, the resulting igneous rock can be classified as intrusive, plutonic, hypabyssal, extrusive, or volcanic. Magma that solidifies at a depth is intrusive, cools slowly, and has a coarse grain as a result. An example is granite. Magma that solidifies at or near the surface is extrusive, cools quickly, and usually has a fine grain. An example is basalt. Magma that actually flows out of the Earth's surface is called lava. Some extrusive rock cools so quickly that crystals do not have time to form. These rocks have a glassy appearance. An example is obsidian. Hypabyssal rock is igneous rock that is formed at medium depths.

Maps

Traditional maps represent land in two dimensions, while topographic maps represent elevation through the use of contour lines. Contour lines help show changes to elevations above the surface of the Earth and on the ocean floor. They also help show the shape of Earth's surface features. The United States Geological Survey (USGS) produces frequently used quadrangle maps in various scales. A quadrangle topographic map is bounded by two lines of latitude and two lines of longitude. A 7.5-minute map shows an area that spans 7.5 minutes of latitude and 7.5 minutes of longitude. The name of the quadrangle map appears at the top, and usually indicates the name of a prominent feature. Topographic maps that show much less detail are also available. They might show a much larger area, such as a country or state. USGS quad maps also refer to adjacent quad maps. Other information contained on quad maps includes the projection and grid used, scale, contour intervals, and magnetic declination, which is the difference between true north and magnetic north.

Mass extinction

Mass extinction, also known as an extinction event, is a decrease in the number of species over a short period of time. While there are many theories as to the causes of mass extinction, it occurs when a relatively large number of species die off or when fewer species evolve than expected. Extinction events are classified as major and minor. It is generally accepted that there have been five major extinction events in Earth's history. The five most significant mass extinction events are Ordovician-Silurian, Permian-Triassic, Late Devonian, Triassic-Jurassic, and Cretaceous-Tertiary.

Uniformitarianism, catastrophism, and superposition

Uniformitarianism: Also known as gradualism, uniformitarianism is the belief among modern geologists that the forces, processes, and laws that we see today have existed throughout geologic time. It involves the belief that the present is the key to the past, and that relatively slow processes have shaped the geological features of Earth. Catastrophism: This is the belief that the Earth was shaped by sudden, short-term catastrophic events.

Superposition: In geology, and in the field of stratigraphy in particular, the law of superposition is that underground layers closer to the surface were deposited more recently.

Geologic time scale

One year is 365.25 days long. The International System of Units (SI) suggests the symbol "a" for a standard year or annum. The prefixes "M" for mega and "G" for giga are used to refer to one million and one billion years, respectively. Ma stands for a megannum (10^6 years) and Ga stands for a gigannum (10^9 years). For example, it can be said that the Earth was formed 4.5 billion years ago, or 4.5 Ga. The term "ago" is understood. Use of the abbreviation "mya" for millions of years (ago) is discouraged, but it is still occasionally used. The abbreviation "BP" stands for "before present." The "present" is defined as January 1, 1950, since present changes from year to year. Another abbreviation used is BCE, which stands for "Before the Common Era." Christian and current can also be used in place of common.

Geologists use the geologic time scale when discussing Earth's chronology and the formation of rocks and minerals. Age is calculated in millions of years before the present time. Units of time are often delineated by geologic or paleontologic events. Smaller units of time such as eras are distinguished by the abundance and/or extinction of certain plant and animal life. For example, the extinction of the dinosaurs marks the end of the Mesozoic era and the beginning of the Cenozoic, the present, era. We are in the Holocene epoch. The supereon encompasses the greatest amount of time. It is composed of eons. Eons are divided into eras, eras into periods, and periods into epochs. Layers of rock also correspond to periods of time in geochronology. Current theory holds that the Earth was formed 4.5 billion years ago.

Development of geologic time scale

The first known observations of stratigraphy were made by Aristotle, who lived before the time of Christ. He observed seashells in ancient rock formations and on the beach, and concluded that the fossilized seashells were similar to current seashells. Avicenna, a Persian scholar from the 11th century, also made early advances in the development of stratigraphy with the concept of superposition. Nicolas Steno, a Danish scientist from the 17th century, expounded upon this with the belief that layers of rock are piled on top of each other. In the 18th century, Abraham Werner categorized rocks from four different periods: the Primary, Secondary, Tertiary, and Quaternary periods. This fell out of use when the belief emerged that rock layers containing the same fossils had been deposited at the same time, and were therefore from the same age. British geologists created the names for many of the time divisions in use today. For example, the Devonian period was named after the county of Devon, and the Permian period was named after Perm, Russia.

Relative and absolute time

A numerical, or "absolute," age is a specific number of years, such as 150 million years ago. A "relative" age refers to a time range, such as the Mesozoic era. It is used to determine whether one rock formation is older or younger than another formation. Radioactive dating is a form of absolute dating and stratigraphy is a form of relative dating. Radioactive dating techniques have provided the most information about the absolute age of rocks and other geological features. Together, geochronologists have created a geologic time scale. Biostratigraphy uses plant and animal fossils within rock to determine its relative age.

Stratigraphy

Stratigraphy is a branch of geology that involves the study of rock layers and layering. Sedimentary rocks are the primary focus of stratigraphy. Subfields include lithostratigraphy, which is the study of the vertical layering of rock types, and biostratigraphy, which is the study of fossil evidence in rock layers. Magnetostratigraphy is the study of changes in detrital remnant magnetism (DRM), which is used to measure the polarity of Earth's magnetic field at the time a stratum was deposited. Chronostratigraphy focuses on the relative dating of rock strata based on the time of rock formation. Unconformity refers to missing layers of rock.

Fossils

Fossils provide a wealth of information about the past, particularly about the flora and fauna that once occupied the Earth, but also about the geologic history of the Earth itself and how Earth and its inhabitants came to be. Some fossilized remains in the geohistorical record exemplify ongoing processes in the Earth's environment, such as weathering, glaciation, and volcanism. These have all led to evolutionary changes in plants and animals. Other fossils support the theory that catastrophic events caused drastic changes in the Earth and its living creatures. One example of this type of theory is that a meteor struck the Earth and caused dinosaurs to become extinct. Both types of fossils provide scientists with a way to hypothesize whether these types of events will happen again.

Fossils are preservations of plants, animals, their remains, or their traces that date back to about 10,000 years ago. Fossils and where they are found in rock strata makes up the fossil record. Fossils are formed under a very specific set of conditions. The fossil must not be damaged by predators and scavengers after death, and the fossil must not decompose. Usually, this happens when the organism is quickly covered with sediment. This sediment builds up and molecules in the organism's body are replaced by minerals. Fossils come in an array of sizes, from single-celled organisms to large dinosaurs.

Atmospheric layers

Earth's atmosphere has five main layers. From lowest to highest, these are the troposphere, the stratosphere, the mesosphere, the thermosphere, and the exosphere. Between each pair of layers is a transition layer called a pause. The troposphere includes the tropopause, which is the transitional layer of the stratosphere. Energy from Earth's surface is transferred to the troposphere. Temperature decreases with altitude in this layer. In the stratosphere, the temperature is inverted, meaning that it increases with altitude. The

- 74 -

stratosphere includes the ozone layer, which helps block ultraviolet light from the Sun. The stratopause is the transitional layer to the mesosphere. The temperature of the mesosphere decreases with height. It is considered the coldest place on Earth, and has an average temperature of -85 degrees Celsius. Temperature increases with altitude in the thermosphere, which includes the thermopause. Just past the thermosphere is the exobase, the base layer of the exosphere. Beyond the five main layers are the ionosphere, homosphere, heterosphere, and magnetosphere.

Earth's atmosphere

The atmosphere consists of 78% nitrogen, 21% oxygen, and 1% argon. It also includes traces of water vapor, carbon dioxide and other gases, dust particles, and chemicals from Earth. The atmosphere becomes thinner the farther it is from the Earth's surface. It becomes difficult to breathe at about 3 km above sea level. The atmosphere gradually fades into space. The lowest layer of the atmosphere is called the troposphere. Its thickness varies at the poles and the equator, varying from about 7 to 17 km. This is where most weather occurs. The stratosphere is next, and continues to an elevation of about 51 km. The mesosphere extends from the stratosphere to an elevation of about 81 km. It is the coldest layer and is where meteors tend to ablate. The next layer is the thermosphere. It is where the International Space Station orbits. The exosphere is the outermost layer, extends to 10,000 km, and mainly consists of hydrogen and helium.

Tropospheric circulation

Most weather takes place in the troposphere. Air circulates in the atmosphere by convection and in various types of "cells." Air near the equator is warmed by the Sun and rises. Cool air rushes under it, and the higher, warmer air flows toward Earth's poles. At the poles, it cools and descends to the surface. It is now under the hot air, and flows back to the equator. Air currents coupled with ocean currents move heat around the planet, creating winds, weather, and climate. Winds can change direction with the seasons. For example, in Southeast Asia and India, summer monsoons are caused by air being heated by the Sun. This air rises, draws moisture from the ocean, and causes daily rains. In winter, the air cools, sinks, pushes the moist air away, and creates dry weather.

Layers above Earth's surface

The ozone layer, although contained within the stratosphere, is determined by ozone (O_3) concentrations. It absorbs the majority of ultraviolet light from the Sun. The ionosphere is part of both the exosphere and the thermosphere. It is characterized by the fact that it is a plasma, a partially ionized gas in which free electrons and positive ions are attracted to each other, but are too energetic to remain fixed as a molecule. It starts at about 50 km above Earth's surface and goes to 1,000 km. It affects radio wave transmission and auroras. The ionosphere pushes against the inner edge of the Earth's magnetosphere, which is the highly magnetized, non-spherical region around the Earth. The homosphere encompasses the troposphere, stratosphere, and mesosphere. Gases in the homosphere are considered well mixed. In the heterosphere, the distance that particles can move without colliding is large. As a result, gases are stratified according to their molecular weights. Heavier gases such as oxygen and nitrogen occur near the bottom of the heterosphere, while hydrogen, the lightest element, is found at the top.

Hydrosphere

Much of Earth is covered by a layer of water or ice called the hydrosphere. Most of the hydrosphere consists of ocean water. The water cycle and the many processes involved in it take place in the hydrosphere. There are several theories regarding how the Earth's hydrosphere was formed. Earth contains more surface water than other planets in the inner solar system. Outgassing, the slow release of trapped water vapor from the Earth's interior, is one theory used to explain the existence of water on Earth. This does not really account for the quantity of water on Earth, however. Another hypothesis is that the early Earth was subjected to a period of bombardment by comets and water-rich asteroids, which resulted in the release of water into the Earth's environment. If this is true, much of the water on the surface of the Earth today originated from the outer parts of the solar system beyond Neptune.

Formation of Earth's atmosphere

It is generally believed that the Earth's atmosphere evolved into its present state. Some believe Earth's early atmosphere contained hydrogen, helium, methane, ammonia, and some water vapor. These elements also played a role in planet formation. Earth's early atmosphere was developed before the emergence of living organisms as we know them today. Eventually, the hot hydrogen and helium escaped Earth's gravity and drifted off. Others believe the early atmosphere contained a large amount of carbon dioxide. Either way, there was probably little oxygen at the time. One theory is that a second stage of the atmosphere evolved over several hundred million years through a process during which methane, ammonia, and water vapor broke down and reformed into nitrogen, hydrogen, and carbon dioxide. About two billion years ago, higher levels of oxygen were found in the atmosphere, which is indicated by large deposits of iron ore. At the same time, iron ores created in oxygen-poor environments stopped forming. The oxygen in the atmosphere today comes mainly from plants and microorganisms such as algae.

Paleozoic era

The Paleozoic era began about 542 Ma and lasted until 251 Ma. It is further divided into six periods. The Paleozoic era began after the supercontinent Pannotia started to break up and at the end of a global ice age. By the end of the era, the supercontinent Pangaea had formed. The beginning of the Paleozoic era is marked by Cambrian Explosion, a time when there were abundant life forms according to the fossil record. The end of the era is marked by one of the major extinction events, the Permian extinction, during which almost 90 percent of the species living at the time became extinct. Many plant and animal forms appeared on the land and in the sea during this era. It is also when large land plants first appeared in the fossil record. There are many invertebrates found in the fossil record of the Paleozoic era, and fish, amphibians, and reptiles also first appeared in the fossil record during this era. There were also large swamps and forests, some of which were formed into coal deposits that exist today.

Earth's formation

Earth's early development began after a supernova exploded. This led to the formation of the Sun out of hydrogen gas and interstellar dust. These same elements swirled around the newly-formed Sun and formed the planets, including Earth. Scientists theorize that about

4.5 billion years ago, Earth was a chunk of rock surrounded by a cloud of gas. It is believed it lacked water and the type of atmosphere that exists today. Heat from radioactive materials in the rock and pressure in the Earth's interior melted the interior. This caused the heavier materials, such as iron, to sink. Lighter silicate-type rocks rose to the Earth's surface. These rocks formed the Earth's earliest crust. Other chemicals also rose to the Earth's surface, helping to form the water and atmosphere. There is one material that has been dated by scientists and found to be 4.4 billion years old. The material is zircon, which consists of zirconium, silicon, and oxygen. Zircon is a mineral that has a high resistance to weathering.

Cenozoic era

The Cenozoic era began about 65.5 Ma and continues to the present. It is marked by the Cretaceous-Tertiary extinction event (extinction of the dinosaurs as well as many invertebrates and plants). The Cenozoic era is further divided into the Paleogene, Neogene, and Quaternary periods. During the Cenozoic era, Pangaea continued to drift, and the plates eventually moved into their present positions. The Pleistocene Ice Age, also known as Quaternary glaciation or the current ice age began about 2.58 Ma and includes the glaciation occurring today. Mammals continued to evolve and other plants and animals came into existence during this era. The fossil record includes the ancestors of the horse, rhinoceros, and camel. It also includes the first dogs and cats and the first humanlike creatures. The first humans appeared less than 200,000 years ago.

Mesozoic era

The Mesozoic era is known as the Age of the Dinosaurs. It is also the era during which the dinosaurs became extinct. The fossil record also shows the appearance of mammals and birds. Trees that existed included gymnosperms, which have uncovered seeds and are mostly cone bearing, and angiosperms, which have covered seeds and are flowering plants. The angiosperm group is currently the dominant plant group. It was also during this era that the supercontinent Pangaea divided into the continental pieces that exist today. During the Cretaceous period, sea levels rose until one-third of the Earth's present land mass was underwater, and then receded. This period created huge marine deposits and chalk. The extinction of the dinosaurs happened about 65 Ma, and was believed to have been triggered by the impact of an asteroid.

Ocean

The ocean is the salty body of water that encompasses the Earth. It has a mass of 1.4×10^{24} grams. Geographically, the ocean is divided into three large oceans: the Pacific Ocean, the Atlantic Ocean, and the Indian Ocean. There are also other divisions, such as gulfs, bays, and various types of seas, including Mediterranean and marginal seas. Ocean distances can be measured by latitude, longitude, degrees, meters, miles, and nautical miles. The ocean accounts for 70.8% of the surface of the Earth, amounting to 361,254,000 km². The ocean's depth is greatest at Challenger Deep in the Mariana Trench. The ocean floor here is 10,924 meters below sea level. The depths of the ocean are mapped by echo sounders and satellite altimeter systems. Echo sounders emit a sound pulse from the surface and record the time it takes to return. Satellite altimeters provide better maps of the ocean floor.

Ocean's importance

The ocean covers 71 percent of the Earth's surface and contains 97 percent of the planet's water. The ocean is an important part of the biosphere, the hydrologic cycle, and tropospheric circulation. It also plays a key role in Earth's weather and climate, which influence the daily lives of humans. The main uses of the ocean and coastal areas for humans are food, transport, oil, gas, and recreation. It is estimated that the ocean provides a means of support for almost 50 percent of all species on Earth. Roughly 20 percent of the animal protein in human diets comes from the ocean.

Seawater

Salinity is a measure of the amount of dissolved salts in ocean water. It is defined in terms of conductivity. Salinity is influenced by the geologic formations in the area, with igneous formations leading to lower salinity and sedimentary formations leading to higher salinity. Dryer areas with greater rates of evaporation also have higher salt concentrations. Areas where fresh water mixes with ocean water have lower salt concentrations. Hydrogen and oxygen make up about 96.5% of sea water. The major constituents of the dissolved solids of sea water at an atomic level are chlorine (55.3%), sodium (30.8%), magnesium (3.7%), sulfur (2.6%), calcium (1.2%), and potassium (1.1%). The salinity of ocean water is fairly constant, ranging from 34.60 to 34.80 parts per thousand, which is 200 parts per million. Measuring variation on this small of a scale requires instruments that are accurate to about one part per million.

Ocean floor

The ocean floor includes features similar to those found on land, such as mountains, ridges, plains, and canyons. The oceanic crust is a thin, dense layer that is about 10 km thick. The greatest volume of water is contained in the basins with lesser volumes that occupy the low-lying areas of the continents, which are known as the continental shelves. The continental slope connects the shelf to the ocean floor of the basin. The continental rise is a slightly sloping area between the slope and the basin. A seamount is an undersea volcanic peak that rises to a height of at least 1,000 meters. A guyot is a seamount with a flat top. A mid-ocean ridge is a continuous undersea mountain chain. Sills are low parts of ridges separating ocean basins or other seas. Trenches are long, narrow troughs. Many isolated peaks and seamounts are scattered throughout the ocean basins, and interrupt ocean currents.

Gyres and the Coriolis effect

Gyres are surface ocean currents that form large circular patterns. In the Northern Hemisphere, they flow clockwise. In the Southern Hemisphere, they flow counterclockwise. These directions are caused by the Coriolis effect. The Coriolis effect occurs due to the fact that the Earth is a rotating object. In the Northern Hemisphere, currents appear to be curving to the right. In the Southern Hemisphere, currents appear to be curving to the left. This is because the Earth is rotating. Gyres tend to flow in the opposite direction near the Earth's poles. In the portion of the Pacific Ocean north of the equator, the major currents are North Pacific, California, North Equatorial, and Kuroshio. In the South Pacific, they are South Equatorial, East Australia, South Pacific, and Peru. In the North Atlantic, they are the North

Atlantic Drift, Canary, North Equatorial, and Gulf Stream. In the South Atlantic, they are South Equatorial, Brazil, South Atlantic, and Benguela.

Ocean currents

Surface currents are caused by winds. Subsurface currents, which occur deep beneath the ocean's surface, are caused by land masses and the Earth's rotation. The density of ocean water can also affect currents. Sea water with a higher salinity is denser than sea water with a lower salinity. Water from denser areas flows to areas with water that is less dense. Currents are classified by temperature. Colder polar sea water flows south towards warmer water, forming cold currents. Warm water currents swirl around the basins and equator. In turn, heat lost and gained by the ocean creates winds. Ocean currents play a significant role in transferring this heat toward the poles, which aids in the development of many types of weather phenomena.

Upwelling and Ekman transport

Upwelling occurs where wind blows parallel to a coast. This causes the ocean surface to move away from the coast. Deep-sea water, which is usually cold and rich in nutrients, rises to takes its place. Ekman transport refers to the impact of the Coriolis effect when wind moves water. Wind blowing in one direction tries to move the surface layer of water in a straight line, but the rotation of the Earth causes water to move in a curved direction. The wind continues to blow the surface of the water and the surface water turns slightly. Below the surface, the water turns even more, eventually creating a spiral. This creates water movement at a right angle to the wind direction. The importance of upwelling is that it brings the nutrient-rich dead and rotting sea creatures closer to the ocean's surface. Here, they are consumed by phytoplankton, which is in turn eaten by zooplankton. Fish eat the zooplankton, and larger creatures and humans eat the fish. Downwelling is the opposite of upwelling.

Deep sea currents

Deep sea currents are often likened to a conveyor belt because they circumnavigate the entire ocean, albeit weakly, and slowly mix deeper and shallower water. In the winter, deep circulation carries cold water from high latitudes to lower latitudes throughout the world. This takes place in areas where most water is at a depth of between 4 and 5 km. This water mass can be as cold as or colder than 4°C. Surface ocean temperatures average about 17°C, but can vary from -2°C to 36°C. The vast cold mass of sea water is also dense and has a high saline content, which forces it to sink at high latitudes. It spreads out, stratifies, and fills the ocean basins. Deep mixing occurs and then the water upwells. The manner in which deep sea currents move can be described as abyssal circulation.

Ocean waves

Most waves in the ocean are formed by winds. The stronger the winds are, the larger the waves will be. The highest point of a wave is the crest. The lowest point of a wave is the trough. The wavelength is measured from crest to crest. The wave height is measured from the trailing trough to the peak of the crest. The wave frequency refers to the number of wave crests passing a designated point each second. A wave period is the time it takes for a wave crest to reach the point of the wave crest of the previous wave. The energy in the wave

- 79 -

runs into the shallow sea floor. This causes the wave to become steeper and then fall over, or break.

Other types of waves

Waves that reach the shore are not all the same size. They can be larger or smaller than average. About once an hour, there is usually a wave that is twice the size of others. There are even larger, but rare, rogue waves, which often travel alone and in a direction different than other waves. Swells are waves that have traveled a great distance. These types of waves are usually large waves with flatter crests. They are very regular in shape and size. The sea level slowly rises and falls over the period of a day. These types of waves on the sea surface are known as tides. Tides have wavelengths of thousands of kilometers. They differ from other wave types in that they are created by slow and very small changes in gravity due to the motion of the Sun and the Moon relative to Earth.

Tsunamis

Seismic sea waves or tsunamis (sometimes mistakenly called tidal waves) are formed by seismic activity. A tsunami is a series of waves with long wavelengths and long periods. Far out at sea, the heights of these waves are typically less than one meter. The wavelength may be 100 km and the wave period may range from five minutes to one hour. However, as seismic sea waves approach the shoreline, the bottom of the wave is slowed down by the shallower sea floor. The top is not slowed as much, and wave height increases to as much as 20 meters. These waves can hit the shore at speeds of up to 30 miles per hour. Tsunamis are caused by earthquakes, submarine landslides, and volcanic eruptions.

Beaufort wind scale

The Beaufort wind scale assigns a numerical value to wind conditions and the appearance of the sea. Zero represents a calm, mirror-like sea with no measurable wind. Twelve is the maximum on the Beaufort scale, and represents hurricane force winds with speeds of 35.2 meters per second (m/s). Visibility is greatly reduced, the sea air is filled with foam, and the sea is completely white with driving spray. The scale is as follows: 1 is light wind with a speed of 1.2 m/s; 2 is a light breeze of 2.8 m/s; 3 is a gentle breeze of 4.9 m/s; 4 is a moderate breeze of 7.7 m/s; and 5 is a fresh breeze of 10.5 m/s. At 5, there are moderate waves, many white caps, and some spray. Six is a strong breeze of 13.1 m/s; 7 is a near gale with wind speeds of 15.8 m/s; 8 is gale force winds of 18.8 m/s; 9 is strong gales of 22.1 m/s; 10 is considered a storm with wind speeds of 25.9 m/s; and 11 is a violent storm.

Shoreline

The area where land meets the sea is called the shoreline. This marks the average position of the ocean. Longshore currents create longshore drift or transport (also called beach drift). This is when ocean waves move toward a beach at an angle, which moves water along the coast. Sediment is eroded from some areas and deposited in others. In this way, it is moved along the beach. Rip currents are strong, fast currents that occur when part of longshore current moves away from the beach. Hard, man-made structures built perpendicular to the beach tend to trap sand on the up-current side. Erosion occurs on the down-current side. Features formed by the sediment deposited by waves include spits, bay-mouth bars, tombolos, barrier islands, and buildups. Sand is composed of weather-resistant, granular materials like quartz and orthoclase. In some locations, it is composed of rock and basalt.

Tides

The gravitational pull of the Sun and Moon causes the oceans to rise and fall each day, creating high and low tides. Most areas have two high tides and two low tides per day. Because the Moon is closer to the Earth than the Sun, its gravitational pull is much greater. The water on the side of the Earth that is closest to the Moon and the water on the opposite side experience high tide. The two low tides occur on the other sides. This changes as the Moon revolves around the Earth. Tidal range is the measurement of the height difference between low and high tide. Tidal range also changes with the location of the Sun and Moon throughout the year, creating spring and neap tides. When all these bodies are aligned, the combined gravitational pull is greater and the tidal range is also greater. This is what creates the spring tide. The neap tide is when the tidal range is at its lowest, which occurs when the Sun and Moon are not at right angles.

Black smokers

Black smokers are a relatively recently discovered feature of the ocean floor. They were first identified in 1977. A black smoker is a type of hydrothermal vent formed when superheated water from below Earth's crust emerges from the ocean floor. This hot water is also rich in sulfides and other minerals from the Earth's crust. When the hot water comes in contact with the cold ocean water, it creates a black chimney-like structure around the vent. Water temperatures around black smokers have been recorded at 400°C. However, water pressure is too great on the sea floor to allow for boiling. The water is also very acidic (twice that of vinegar). It is estimated that the yearly volume of water passing through black smokers is 1.4×10^{14} kg.

Carbon cycle

The carbon and nutrient cycles of the ocean are processes that are due in part to the deep currents, mixing, and upwelling that occur in the ocean. Carbon dioxide (CO_2) from the atmosphere is dissolved into the ocean at higher latitudes and distributed to the denser deep water. Where upwelling occurs, CO_2 is brought back to the surface and emitted into the tropical air. Phytoplankton are typically single-celled organisms that are nourished by the Sun. They are photosynthetic autotrophs, meaning they convert water, carbon dioxide, and solar energy into food. They drift with the currents, produce oxygen as a byproduct, and serve as a food source. Zooplankton feed on phytoplankton. Zooplankton are heterotrophic organisms, meaning they do not synthesize their own food. Zooplankton can be single-celled creatures or much larger organisms, such as jellyfish, mollusks, and crustaceans.

El Niño-Southern Oscillation (ENSO)

The El Niño-Southern Oscillation (ENSO) is a climate pattern of the Pacific Ocean area that lasts 6 to 18 months and causes weather that is different from the expected seasonal patterns and variations. There are two sets of events associated with ENSO: El Niño and La Niña. The usual weather patterns for the Pacific Ocean involve the movement of sea water by winds from the eastern part of the tropical Pacific to the western part of the Pacific Ocean. This pattern causes cold deep water upwells in the eastern Pacific. This creates wet weather and is considered a low-pressure system. Conversely, the eastern Pacific is a dry, high-pressure system. El Niño weakens upwelling because equalization in air pressure leads to less wind, which leads to more water staying in the eastern Pacific. La Niña increases upwelling because winds grow stronger because of higher air pressures across the Pacific. Both El Niño and La Niña cause extreme weather events such as droughts, heavy rain, and flooding.

Rift valley

Rift valleys occur both on land and in the ocean. They are a result of plate tectonics, and occur when plates are spreading apart. In the ocean, this is part of the crust development cycle in which new crust is created at mid-ocean ridges and old crust is lost at the trenches. The Mid-Atlantic Ridge is an example of this. It occurs at divergent Eurasian and North American plates and in the South Atlantic, African, and South American plates. The East Pacific Rise is also a mid-oceanic ridge. The most extensive rift valley is located along the crest of the mid-ocean ridge system. It is a result of sea floor spreading.

Beaches

Weathering erodes the parent material of beaches, rock and soil, into sand, which is typically quartz. Other parts of the soil such as clay and silt are deposited in areas of the continental shelf. The larger sand particles get deposited in the form of a beach. This includes a near shore, which is underwater, a fore shore, the area typically considered the beach, and a back shore. The offshore starts about 5 meters from the shoreline and extends to about 20 meters. The beach also includes wet and dry parts and a fore dune and rear dune. Waves typically move sand from the sea to the beach, and gravity and wave action move it back again. Wind gradually pushes sand particles uphill in a jumping motion called saltation. Sand stays deposited in the form of dunes and the dunes appear as if they roll backward. Storms can both erode a beach and provide additional deposition.

North Atlantic Oscillation (NAO)

The North Atlantic Oscillation is a climatic occurrence that affects winter weather in the Northern Hemisphere, particularly in the east coast regions of the United States, Europe, and North Africa. Atmospheric pressure over the North Atlantic caused by the Icelandic Low and the high pressure Azores leads to the North Atlantic Oscillation. There is both a "positive" and "negative" phase of the NAO. The positive phase is when strong winds caused by a large difference in air pressure send wet winter storms from eastern North America to northern Europe. Weaker winds associated with a smaller difference in air pressure cause eastern North America and northern Europe to have fewer winter storms. Instead, the weather is rainy in southern Europe and North Africa.

Weather, climate, and meteorology

Meteorology is the study of the atmosphere, particularly as it pertains to forecasting the weather and understanding its processes. Weather is the condition of the atmosphere at any given moment. Most weather occurs in the troposphere. Weather includes changing events such as clouds, storms, and temperature, as well as more extreme events such as tornadoes, hurricanes, and blizzards. Climate refers to the average weather for a particular area over time, typically at least 30 years. Latitude is an indicator of climate. Changes in climate occur over long time periods.

Weather phenomena

Common atmospheric conditions that are frequently measured are temperature, precipitation, wind, and humidity. These weather conditions are often measured at permanently fixed weather stations so weather data can be collected and compared over time and by region. Measurements may also be taken by ships, buoys, and underwater instruments. Measurements may also be taken under special circumstances. The measurements taken include temperature, barometric pressure, humidity, wind speed, wind direction, and precipitation. Usually, the following instruments are used: A thermometer is used for measuring temperature; a barometer is used for measuring barometric/air pressure; a hygrometer is used for measuring humidity; an anemometer is used for measuring wind speed; a weather vane is used for measuring wind direction; and a rain gauge is used for measuring precipitation.

Latitudinal variation of solar radiation

Latitude is a measurement of the distance from the equator. The distance from the equator indicates how much solar radiation a particular area receives. The equator receives more sunlight, while polar areas receive less. The Earth tilts slightly on its rotational axis. This tilt determines the seasons and affects weather. There are eight biomes or ecosystems with particular climates that are associated with latitude. Those in the high latitudes, which get the least sunlight, are tundra and taiga. Those in the mid latitudes are grassland, temperate forest, and chaparral. Those in latitudes closest to the equator are the warmest. The biomes are desert and tropical rain forest. The eighth biome is the ocean, which is unique because it consists of water and spans the entire globe. Insolation refers to incoming solar radiation. Diurnal variations refer to the daily changes in insolation. The greatest insolation occurs at noon.

Tilt of the Earth

The tilt of the Earth on its axis is 23.5°. This tilt causes the seasons and affects the temperature because it affects the amount of Sun the area receives. When the Northern or Southern Hemispheres are tilted toward the Sun, the hemisphere tilted toward the sun experiences summer and the other hemisphere experiences winter. This reverses as the Earth revolves around the Sun. Fall and spring occur between the two extremes. The equator gets the same amount of sunlight every day of the year, about 12 hours, and doesn't experience seasons. Both poles have days during the winter when they are tilted away from the Sun and receive no daylight. The opposite effect occurs during the summer. There are 24 hours of daylight and no night. The summer solstice, the day with the most amount of sunlight, occurs on June 21st in the Northern Hemisphere and on December 21st in the Southern Hemisphere. The winter solstice, the day with the least amount of sunlight, occurs on December 21st in the Northern Hemisphere and on June 21st in the Southern Hemisphere.

Breezes

Sea breezes and land breezes help influence an area's prevailing winds, particularly in areas where the wind flow is light. Sea breezes, also called onshore breezes, are the result of the different capacities for absorbing heat of the ocean and the land. The sea can be warmed to a greater depth than the land. It warms up more slowly than the land's surface. Land heats air above it as its temperature increases. This heated; warmer is less dense and rises as a result. The cooler air above the sea and higher sea level pressure create a wind flow in the direction of the land. Coastal areas often receive these cooler breezes. Land cools slower at night than the ocean, and coastal breezes weaken at this time. When the land becomes so cool that it is cooler than the sea surface, the pressure over the ocean is lower than the land. This creates a land breeze. This can cause rain and thunderstorms over the ocean.

Wind

Winds are the result of air moving by convection. Masses of warm air rise, and cold air sweeps into their place. The warm air also moves, cools, and sinks. The term "prevailing wind" refers to the wind that usually blows in an area in a single direction. Dominant winds are the winds with the highest speeds. Belts or bands that run latitudinally and blow in a specific direction are associated with convection cells. Hadley cells are formed directly north and south of the equator. The Farrell cells occur at about 30° to 60°. The jet stream runs between the Farrell cells and the polar cells. At the higher and lower latitudes, the direction is easterly. At mid latitudes, the direction is westerly. From the North Pole to the south, the surface winds are Polar High Easterlies, Subpolar Low Westerlies, Subtropical High or Horse Latitudes, North-East Trade winds, Equatorial Low or Doldrums, South-East Trades, Subtropical High or Horse Latitudes, Subpolar Low Easterlies, and Polar High.

Thunderstorms

A thunderstorm is one of the many weather phenomena that can be created during the ongoing process of heat moving through Earth's atmosphere. Thunderstorms form when there is moisture to form rain clouds, unstable air, and lift. Unstable air is usually caused by warm air rising quickly through cold air. Lift can be caused by fronts, sea breezes, and elevated terrain, such as mountains. Single cell thunderstorms have one main draft. Multicell clusters have clusters of storms. Multicell lines have severe thunderstorms along a squall line. Supercell thunderstorms are large and severe, and have the capacity to produce destructive tornadoes. Thunder is a sonic shock wave caused by the rapid expansion of air around lightning. Lightning is the discharge of electricity during a thunderstorm. Lightning can also occur during volcanic eruptions or dust storms.

Atmospheric variations

Terrain affects several local atmospheric conditions, including temperature, wind speed, and wind direction. When there are land forms, heating of the ground can be greater than the heating of the surrounding air than it would be at the same altitude above sea level. This creates a thermal low in the region and amplifies any existing thermal lows. It also changes the wind circulation. Terrain such as hills and valleys increase friction between the air and the land, which disturbs the air flow. This physical block deflects the wind, and the resulting air flow is called a barrier jet. Just as the heating of the land and air affect sea and land

- 84 -

breezes along the coast, rugged terrain affects the wind circulation between mountains and valleys.

Cyclones

Cyclones generally refer to large air masses rotating in the same direction as the Earth. They are formed in low pressure areas. Cyclones vary in size. Some are mesoscale systems, which vary in size from about 5 km to hundreds of kilometers. Some are synoptic scale systems, which are about 1,000 km in size. The size of subtropical cyclones is somewhere in between. Cold-core polar and extratropical cyclones are synoptic scale systems. Warm-core tropical, polar low and mesocyclones are mesoscale systems. Extratropical cyclones, sometimes called mid-latitude cyclones or wave cyclones, occur in the middle latitudes. They have neither tropical nor polar characteristics. Extratropical cyclones are everyday phenomena which, along with anticyclones, drive the weather over much of the Earth. They can produce cloudiness, mild showers, heavy gales, and thunderstorms. Anticyclones occur when there is a descending pocket of air of higher than average pressure. Anticyclones are usually associated with clearing skies and drier, cooler air.

Tornados

During a tornado, wind speeds can be upward of 300 miles per hour. Tornados are rotating funnel-like clouds. They have a very high energy density, which means they are very destructive to a small area. They are also short-lived. About 75% of the world's tornadoes occur in the United States, mostly in an area of the Great Plains known as Tornado Alley. If there are two or more columns of air, it is referred to as a multiple vortex tornado. A satellite tornado is a weak tornado that forms near a larger one within the same mesocyclone. A waterspout is a tornado over water. The severity of tornadoes is measured using the Enhanced Fujita Scale. An EF-0 rating is associated with a 3-second wind gust between 65 and 85 miles per hour, while an EF-5 is associated with wind speeds of greater than 200 mph.

Humidity

Humidity refers to water vapor contained in the air. The amount of moisture contained in air depends upon its temperature. The higher the air temperature, the more moisture it can hold. These higher levels of moisture are associated with higher humidity. Absolute humidity refers to the total amount of moisture air is capable of holding at a certain temperature. Relative humidity is the ratio of water vapor in the air compared to the amount the air is capable of holding at its current temperature. As temperature decreases, absolute humidity stays the same and relative humidity increases. A hygrometer is a device used to measure humidity. The dew point is the temperature at which water vapor condenses into water at a particular humidity.

Hurricanes

A hurricane is one of the three weather phenomena that can occur as a result of a tropical cyclone. A tropical cyclone is a warm-core, low-pressure condition that circles in the same direction as the Earth. A tropical depression has sustained winds of up to 30 miles per hour (mph), with rotational winds around a center. A tropical storm appears more circular and has more rotation than a tropical depression. Its winds range from 39 to 73 mph. A hurricane appears well-organized and sometimes has a recognizable eye with strong rotation. Its wind speed is more than 73 mph. Hurricanes are classified using the Saffir-Simpson Scale, which ranges from category 1 to category 5. A category 5 hurricane has wind speeds greater than 155 mph. Hurricanes are named alphabetically through the season starting with "A." The letters "Q," "U," and "Z" are not used. There are six lists of names that are used from year to year. The names of devastating hurricanes are retired from the list.

Precipitation

After clouds reach the dew point, precipitation occurs. Precipitation can take the form of a liquid or a solid. It is known by many names, including rain, snow, ice, dew, and frost. Liquid forms of precipitation include rain and drizzle. Rain or drizzle that freezes on contact is known as freezing rain or freezing drizzle. Solid or frozen forms of precipitation include snow, ice needles or diamond dust, sleet or ice pellets, hail, and graupel or snow pellets. Virga is a form of precipitation that evaporates before reaching the ground. It usually looks like sheets or shafts falling from a cloud. The amount of rainfall is measured with a rain gauge. Intensity can be measured according to how fast precipitation is falling or by how severely it limits visibility. Precipitation plays a major role in the water cycle since it is responsible for depositing much of the Earth's fresh water.

Heat waves

A heat wave is a stretch of hotter than normal weather. Some heat waves may involve high humidity and last longer than a week. Heat waves can form if a warm high-pressure weather system stalls in an area. The jet stream is a flow that moves air through the middle latitudes. When this shifts, it can bring a pattern of unusually warm weather into a region, creating a heat wave. Heat can be trapped by cities. If there is no rain or clouds to help cool the weather, the heat wave can linger. In humans, heat waves can lead to heat stroke, heat exhaustion, cramps, dehydration, and even death. Plants can dry up and crops can fail. There is also a greater threat of fires during a heat wave in dry areas.

Cloud types

Most clouds can be classified according to the altitude of their base above Earth's surface. High clouds occur at altitudes between 5,000 and 13,000 meters. Middle clouds occur at altitudes between 2,000 and 7,000 meters. Low clouds occur from the Earth's surface to altitudes of 2,000 meters. Types of high clouds include cirrus (Ci), thin wispy mare's tails that consist of ice; cirrocumulus (Cc), small, pillow-like puffs that often appear in rows; and cirrostratus (Cs), thin, sheetlike clouds that often cover the entire sky. Types of middle clouds include altocumulus (Ac), gray-white clouds that consist of liquid water; and altostratus (As), grayish or blue-gray clouds that span the sky. Types of low clouds include stratus (St), gray and fog-like clouds consisting of water droplets that take up the whole sky; stratocumulus (Sc), low-lying, lumpy gray clouds; and nimbostratus (Ns), dark gray clouds with uneven bases that indicate rain or snow. Two types of clouds, cumulus (Cu) and cumulonimbus (Cb), are capable of great vertical growth. They can start at a wide range of altitudes, from the Earth's surface to altitudes of 13,000 meters.

Cloud formation

Clouds form when air cools and warm air is forced to give up some of its water vapor because it can no longer hold it. This vapor condenses and forms tiny droplets of water or ice crystals called clouds. Particles, or aerosols, are needed for water vapor to form water droplets. These are called condensation nuclei. Clouds are created by surface heating, mountains and terrain, rising air masses, and weather fronts. Clouds precipitate, returning the water they contain to Earth. Clouds can also create atmospheric optics. They can scatter light, creating colorful phenomena such as rainbows, colorful sunsets, and the green flash phenomenon.

Air masses and weather fronts

Air masses are large volumes of air in the troposphere of the Earth. They are categorized by their temperature and by the amount of water vapor they contain. Arctic and Antarctic air masses are cold, polar air masses are cool, and tropical and equatorial air masses are hot. Other types of air masses include maritime and monsoon, both of which are moist and unstable. There are also continental and superior air masses, which are dry. A weather front separates two masses of air of different densities. It is the principal cause of meteorological phenomena. Air masses are quickly and easily affected by the land they are above. They can have certain characteristics, and then develop new ones when they get blown over a different area.

Nonstandard cloud types

Contrails, or condensation trails, are thin white streaks caused by jets. These are created from water vapor condensing and freezing the jet's exhaust particles. Contrails can be further classified as short-lived, persistent non-spreading, and persistent. Lenticular or lee wave, clouds are created by an air current over an obstacle, such as a mountain. They appear to be stationary, but are actually forming, dissipating, and reforming in the same place. Kelvin-Helmholtz clouds are formed by winds with different speeds or directions. They look like ocean waves. Mammatus clouds hang down from the base of a cloud, usually a cumulonimbus cloud. They often occur during the warmer months.

Pressure systems

The concept of atmospheric pressure involves the idea that air exerts a force. An imaginary column of air 1 square inch in size rising through the atmosphere would exert a force of 14.7 pounds per square inch (psi). Both temperature and altitude affect atmospheric pressure. Low and high pressure systems tend to want to equalize. Air tends to move from areas of high pressure to areas of low pressure. When air moves into a low pressure system, the air that was there gets pushed up, creating lower temperatures and pressures. Water vapor condenses and forms clouds and possibly rain and snow. A barometer is used to measure air pressure.

Bergeron system

The Bergeron classification system uses three sets of letters to identify the following characteristics of air masses: moisture content, thermal characteristics from where they originated, and the stability of the atmosphere. The first, moisture content, uses the following letters: "c" represents the dry continental air masses and "m" stands for the moist maritime air masses. The second set of abbreviations are as follows: "T" indicates the air mass is tropical in origin; "P" indicates the air mass is polar in origin; "A" indicates the air mass is Antarctic in origin; "M" stands for monsoon; "E" indicates the air mass is equatorial in origin; and "S" is used to represent superior air, which is dry air formed by a downward motion. The last set of symbols provides an indicator of the stability of the mass. "K" indicates the mass is colder than the ground below it, while "w" indicates the mass is warmer than the ground. For example, cP is a continental polar air mass, while cPk is a polar air mass blowing over the Gulf Stream, which is warmer than the mass.

Frontal systems

A cold front is a mass of cold air, usually fast moving and dense, that moves into a warm air front, producing clouds. This often produces a temperature drop and rain, hail (frozen rain), thunder, and lightning. A warm front is pushed up by a fast moving cold front. It is often associated with high wispy clouds, such as cirrus and cirrostratus clouds. A stationary front forms when a warm and cold front meet, but neither is strong enough to move the other. Winds blowing parallel to the fronts keep the front stationary. The front may remain in the same place for days until the wind direction changes and both fronts become a single warm or cold front. In other cases, the entire front dissipates. An occluded front is when a cold front pushes into a warm front. The warm air rises and the two masses of cool air join. These types of fronts often occur in areas of low atmospheric pressure.

Weather fronts and maps

A weather front is the area between two differing masses of air that affects weather. Frontal movements are influenced by the jet stream and other high winds. Movements are determined by the type of front. Cold fronts move up to twice as fast as warm ones. It is in the turbulent frontal area that commonplace and dramatic weather events take place. This area also creates temperature changes. Weather phenomena include rain, thunderstorms, high winds, tornadoes, cloudiness, clear skies, and hurricanes. Different fronts can be plotted on weather maps using a set of designated symbols. Surface weather maps can also include symbols representing clouds, rain, temperature, air pressure, and fair weather.

Cold fronts are represented on weather maps as a blue line. Solid blue triangles are used to indicate the direction of movement. Warm fronts are represented with a red line. Solid red semi-circles are used to indicate the direction of the front. The cold and warm front symbols are merged and alternated to point in opposite directions to indicate a stationary front. An occluded front is represented by a purple line with alternating solid purple triangles and semi-circles. A surface trough is represented by an orange dashed line. A squall or shear line is represented by a red line. Two dots and a dash are alternated to form the line. A dry line is represented by an orange line with semi-circles in outline form. A tropical wave is represented by a straight orange line. An "L" is used to indicate an area of low atmospheric pressure and an "H" is used to indicate an area of high atmospheric pressure.

Weather phenomena

Shearline: This evolves from a stationary front that has gotten smaller. Wind direction shifts over a short distance.

Dry line or dew point line: This separates two warm air masses of differing moisture content. At lower altitudes, the moist air mass wedges under the drier air. At higher altitudes, the dry air wedges under the moist air. This is a frequent occurrence in the Midwest and Canada, where the dry air of the Southwest and the moister air of the Gulf of Mexico meet. This can lead to extreme weather events, including tornadoes and thunderstorms.

Squall line: Severe thunderstorms can form at the front of or ahead of a cold front. In some cases, severe thunderstorms can also outrun cold fronts. A squall line can produce extreme weather in the form of heavy rain, hail, lightning, strong winds, tornadoes, and waterspouts.

Tropical waves or easterly waves: These are atmospheric troughs or areas of low air pressure that travel westward in the tropics, causing clouds and thunderstorms.

Weather forecasting

Short and long-term weather forecasting is important because the day-to-day weather greatly affects humans and human activity. Severe weather and natural events can cause devastating harm to humans, property, and sources of livelihood, such as crops. The persistence method of forecasting can be used to create both short and long-term forecasts in areas that change very little or change slowly. It assumes that the weather tomorrow will be similar to the weather today. Barometric pressure is measured because a change in air pressure can indicate the arrival of a cold front that could lead to precipitation. Long-term forecasts based on climate data are useful to help people prepare for seasonal changes and severe events such as hurricanes.

Astronomy

Astronomy is the scientific study of celestial objects and their positions, movements, and structures. Celestial does not refer to the Earth in particular, but does include its motions as it moves through space. Other objects include the Sun, the Moon, planets, satellites, asteroids, meteors, comets, stars, galaxies, the universe, and other space phenomena. The term astronomy has its roots in the Greek words "astro" and "nomos," which means "laws of the stars."

Universe structure

What can be seen of the universe is believed to be at least 93 billion light years across. To put this into perspective, the Milky Way galaxy is about 100,000 light years across. Our view of matter in the universe is that it forms into clumps. Matter is organized into stars, galaxies, clusters of galaxies, superclusters, and the Great Wall of galaxies. Galaxies consist of stars, some with planetary systems. Some estimates state that the universe is about 13 billion years old. It is not considered dense, and is believed to consist of 73 percent dark energy, 23 percent cold dark matter, and 4 percent regular matter. Cosmology is the study of the universe. Interstellar medium (ISM) is the gas and dust in the interstellar space between a galaxy's stars.

Universe origin

The universe can be said to consist of everything and nothing. The universe is the source of everything we know about space, matter, energy, and time. There are likely still phenomena that have yet to be discovered. The universe can also be thought of as nothing, since a vast portion of the known universe is empty space. It is believed that the universe is expanding. The Big Bang theory, which is widely accepted among astronomers, was developed to explain the origin of the universe. There are other theories regarding the origin of the universe, such as the Steady-State theory and the Creationist theory. The Big Bang theory states that all the matter in the universe was once in one place. This matter underwent a huge explosion that spread the matter into space. Galaxies formed from this material and the universe is still expanding.

Stars

Black hole: A black hole is a space where the gravitational field is so powerful that everything, including light, is pulled into it. Once objects enter the surface, the event horizon, they cannot escape.

Quasar: Quasar stands for quasi-stellar radio source, which is an energetic galaxy with an active galactic nucleus. Quasars were first identified by their emissions of large amounts of electromagnetic energy, such as radio waves and visible light. These emissions differed from those associated with other galaxies.

Blazar: A blazar is a very violent phenomenon in galaxies with supermassive black holes.

Dark matter: Although its existence has not yet been proven, dark matter may account for a large proportion of the universe's mass. It is undetectable because it does not emit any radiation, but is believed to exist because of gravitational forces exerted on visible objects.

Galaxies

Galaxies consist of stars, stellar remnants, and dark matter. Dwarf galaxies contain as few as 10 million stars, while giant galaxies contain as many as 1 trillion stars. Galaxies are gravitationally bound, meaning the stars, star systems, other gases, and dust orbits the galaxy's center. The Earth exists in the Milky Way galaxy and the nearest galaxy to ours is the Andromeda galaxy. Galaxies can be classified by their visual shape into elliptical, spiral, irregular, and starburst galaxies. It is estimated that there are more than 100 billion galaxies in the universe ranging from 1,000 to 100,000 parsecs in diameter. Galaxies can be megaparsecs apart. Intergalactic space consists of a gas with an average density of less than one atom per cubic meter. Galaxies are organized into clusters which form superclusters. Dark matter may account for up to 90% of the mass of galaxies. Dark matter is still not well understood.

Time measurements

A sidereal day is four minutes shorter than a solar day. A solar day is the time it takes the Earth to complete one revolution and face the Sun again. From noon to noon is 24 hours. A sidereal day is measured against a distant "fixed" star. As the Earth completes one rotation, it has also completed part of its revolution around the Sun, so it completes a sidereal rotation in reference to the fixed star before it completes a solar rotation. The Sun travels along the ecliptic in 365.25 days. This can be tracked day after day before dawn. After one year, the stars appear back in their original positions. As a result, different constellations are viewable at different times of the year. Sidereal years are slightly longer than tropical years. The difference is caused by the precession of the equinoxes. A calendar based on the sidereal year will be out of sync with the seasons at a rate of about one day every 71 years.

Large units of distance

An astronomical unit, also known as AU, is a widely used measurement in astronomy. One AU is equal to the distance from the Earth to the Sun, which is 150 million km, or 93 million miles. These distances can also be expressed as 149.60×10^9 m or 92.956×10^6 mi. A light year (ly) is the distance that light travels in a vacuum in one year. A light year is equal to about 10 trillion km, or 64,341 AU, and is used to measure large astronomical units. Also used for measuring large distances is the parsec (pc), which is the preferred unit since it is better suited for recording observational data. A parsec is the parallax of one arcsecond, and is about 31 trillion km (about 19 trillion miles), or about 3.26 light years. It is used to calculate distances by triangulation. The AU distance from the Earth to the Sun is used to form the side of a right triangle.

Star life cycle

There are different life cycle possibilities for stars after they initially form and enter into the main sequence stage. Small, relatively cold red dwarfs with relatively low masses burn hydrogen slowly, and will remain in the main sequence for hundreds of billions of years. Massive, hot supergiants will leave the main sequence after just a few million years. The Sun is a mid-sized star that may be in the main sequence for 10 billion years. After the main sequence, the star expands to become a red giant. Depending upon the initial mass of the star, it can become a black dwarf (from a medium-sized star), and then a small, cooling white dwarf. Massive stars become red supergiants (and sometimes blue supergiants), explode in a supernova, and then become neutron stars. The largest stars can become black holes.

Star birth

A nebula is a cloud of dust and gas that is composed primarily of hydrogen (97%) and helium (3%). Gravity causes parts of the nebula to clump together. This accretion continues adding atoms to the center of an unstable protostar. Equilibrium between gravity pulling atoms and gas pressure pushing heat and light away from the center is achieved. A star dies when it is no longer able to maintain equilibrium. A protostar may never become a star if it does not reach a critical core temperature. It may become a brown dwarf or a gas giant instead. If nuclear fusion of hydrogen into helium begins, a star is born. The "main sequence" of a star's life involves nuclear fusion reactions. During this time, the star contracts over billions of years to compensate for the heat and light energy lost. In the star's core, temperature, density, and pressure increase as the star contracts and the cycle continues.

Hertzsprung-Russell diagram

A Hertzsprung-Russell diagram (H-R diagram or HRD) is a plot or scattergraph depicting stars' temperatures and comparing them with stars' luminosities or magnitudes. This can help determine the age and evolutionary state of a star. A Hertzsprung-Russell diagram is also known as a color-magnitude diagram (CMD). It helps represent the life cycles of stars. In these plots, temperatures are plotted from highest to lowest, which aids in the comparison of H-R diagrams and observations. Hertzsprung-Russell diagrams can have many variations. Most of the stars in these diagrams lie along the line called main sequence, which contains stars that are fusing hydrogen. Other groupings include white dwarfs, subgiants, giants, and supergiants.

Spectral classification

Stars use the Morgan-Keenan classification system, which is based on spectral traits that indicate the ionization of the chromosphere. The following letter designations are used to indicate temperature, from hottest to coolest: O, B, A, F, G, K, and M. The phrase "Oh, be a fine girl/guy, kiss me" can be used as a memory aid. Different types of stars also have different corresponding colors. O stars are blue; A stars are white; G stars are yellow; and M stars are red. The numbers 0 to 9 are used to indicate tenths between two star classes. Zero indicates 0/10 and 9 indicates 9/10. Luminosity output is an indicator of size, and is expressed with the Roman numerals I, II, III, IV, and V. Supergiants are included in class I, giants are included in class III, and main sequence stars are included in class V. Using the Sun as an example, the spectral type G2V could be expressed as "a yellow two-tenths towards an orange main sequence star."

Sun

The Sun is at the center of the solar system. It is composed of 70% hydrogen (H) and 28% helium (He). The remaining 2% is made up of metals. The Sun is one of 100 billion stars in the Milky Way galaxy. Its diameter is 1,390,000 km, its mass is 1.989×10^{30} kg, its surface temperature is 5,800 K, and its core temperature is 15,600,000 K. The Sun represents more than 99.8% of the total mass of the solar system. At the core, the temperature is 15.6 million K, the pressure is 250 billion atmospheres, and the density is more than 150 times that of water. The surface is called the photosphere. The chromosphere lies above this, and the corona, which extends millions of kilometers into space, is next. Sunspots are relatively cool regions on the surface with a temperature of 3,800 K. Temperatures in the corona are over 1,000,000 K. Its magnetosphere, or heliosphere, extends far beyond Pluto.

Solar system formation

A planetary system consists of the various non-stellar objects orbiting a star, such as planets, dwarf planets, moons, asteroids, meteoroids, comets, and cosmic dust. The Sun, together with its planetary system, which includes Earth, is known as the solar system. The theory of how the solar system was created is that it started with the collapse of a cloud of interstellar gas and dust, which formed the solar nebula. This collapse is believed to have occurred because the cloud was disturbed. As it collapsed, it heated up and compressed at the center, forming a flatter protoplanetary disk with a protostar at the center. Planets formed as a result of accretion from the disk. Gas cooled and condensed into tiny particles of rock, metal, and ice. These particles collided and formed into larger particles, and then into object the size of small asteroids. Eventually, some became large enough to have significant gravity.

Solar system components

The solar system is a planetary system of objects that exist in an ecliptic plane. Objects orbit around and are bound by gravity to a star called the Sun. Objects that orbit around the Sun include: planets, dwarf planets, moons, asteroids, meteoroids, cosmic dust, and comets. The definition of planets has changed. At one time, there were nine planets in the solar system. There are now eight. Planetary objects in the solar system include four inner, terrestrial planets: Mercury, Venus, Earth, and Mars. They are relatively small, dense, rocky, lack rings, and have few or no moons. The four outer, or Jovian, planets are Jupiter, Saturn, Uranus, and Neptune, which are large and have low densities, rings, and moons. They are also known as gas giants. Between the inner and outer planets is the asteroid belt. Beyond Neptune is the Kuiper belt. Within these belts are five dwarf planets: Ceres, Pluto, Haumea, Makemake, and Eris.

Sun's energy

The Sun's energy is produced by nuclear fusion reactions. Each second, about 700,000,000 tons of hydrogen are converted (or fused) to about 695,000,000 tons of helium and 5,000,000 tons of energy in the form of gamma rays. In nuclear fusion, four hydrogen nuclei are fused into one helium nucleus, resulting in the release of energy. In the Sun, the energy proceeds towards the surface and is absorbed and re-emitted at lower and lower temperatures. Energy is mostly in the form of visible light when it reaches the surface. It is estimated that the Sun has used up about half of the hydrogen at its core since its birth. It is expected to radiate in this fashion for another 5 billion years. Eventually, it will deplete its hydrogen fuel, grow brighter, expand to about 260 times its diameter, and become a red giant. The outer layers will ablate and become a dense white dwarf the size of the Earth.

Inner terrestrial planets

Mercury: Mercury is the closest to the Sun and is also the smallest planet. It orbits the Sun every 88 days, has no satellites or atmosphere, has a Moon-like surface with craters, appears bright, and is dense and rocky with a large iron core.

Venus: Venus is the second planet from the Sun. It orbits the Sun every 225 days, is very bright, and is similar to Earth in size, gravity, and bulk composition. It has a dense atmosphere composed of carbon dioxide and some sulfur. It is covered with reflective clouds made of sulfuric acid and exhibits signs of volcanism. Lightning and thunder have been recorded on Venus's surface.

Earth: Earth is the third planet from the Sun. It orbits the Sun every 365 days. Approximately 71% of its surface is salt-water oceans. The Earth is rocky, has an atmosphere composed mainly of oxygen and nitrogen, has one moon, and supports millions of species. It contains the only known life in the solar system.

Mars: Mars it the fourth planet from the Sun. It appears reddish due to iron oxide on the surface, has a thin atmosphere, has a rotational period similar to Earth's, and has seasonal cycles. Surface features of Mars include volcanoes, valleys, deserts, and polar ice caps. Mars

- 93 -

has impact craters and the tallest mountain, largest canyon, and perhaps the largest impact crater yet discovered.

Solar system size

The Earth is about 12,765 km (7,934 miles) in diameter. The Moon is about 3,476 km (2,160 mi) in diameter. The distance between the Earth and the Moon is about 384,401 km (238,910 mi). The diameter of the Sun is approximately 1,390,000 km (866,000 mi). The distance from the Earth to the Sun is 149,598,000 km, also known as 1 Astronomical Unit (AU). The star that is nearest to the solar system is Proxima Centauri. It is about 270,000 AU away. Some distant galaxies are so far away that their light takes several billion years to reach the Earth. In other words, people on Earth see them as they looked billions of years ago.

Oort Cloud, asteroid belt, and Kuiper Belt

The asteroid belt is between Mars and Jupiter. The many objects contained within are composed of rock and metal similar to those found on the terrestrial planets. The Kuiper Belt is beyond Neptune's orbit, but the influence of the gas giants may cause objects from the Kuiper Belt to cross Neptune's orbit. Objects in the Kuiper Belt are still being discovered. They are thought to be composed of the frozen forms of water, ammonia, and methane, and may be the source of short-period comets. It is estimated that there are 35,000 Kuiper Belt objects greater than 100 km in diameter and perhaps 100 million objects about 20 km in diameter. There is also a hypothetical Oort Cloud that may exist far beyond the Kuiper Belt and act as a source for long-period comets.

Outer planets

Jupiter: Jupiter is the fifth planet from the Sun and the largest planet in the solar system. It consists mainly of hydrogen, and 25% of its mass is made up of helium. It has a fast rotation and has clouds in the tropopause composed of ammonia crystals that are arranged into bands sub-divided into lighter-hued zones and darker belts causing storms and turbulence. Jupiter has wind speeds of 100 m/s, a planetary ring, 63 moons, and a Great Red Spot, which is an anticyclonic storm.

Saturn: Saturn is the sixth planet from the Sun and the second largest planet in the solar system. It is composed of hydrogen, some helium, and trace elements. Saturn has a small core of rock and ice, a thick layer of metallic hydrogen, a gaseous outer layer, wind speeds of up to 1,800 km/h, a system of rings, and 61 moons.

Uranus: Uranus is the seventh planet from the Sun. Its atmosphere is composed mainly of hydrogen and helium, and also contains water, ammonia, methane, and traces of hydrocarbons. With a minimum temperature of 49 K, Uranus has the coldest atmosphere. Uranus has a ring system, a magnetosphere, and 13 moons.

Neptune: Neptune is the eighth planet from the Sun and is the planet with the third largest mass. It has 12 moons, an atmosphere similar to Uranus, a Great Dark Spot, and the strongest sustained winds of any planet (wind speeds can be as high as 2,100 km/h). Neptune is cold (about 55 K) and has a fragmented ring system.

Meteors, meteoroids, and meteorites

A meteoroid is the name for a rock from space before it enters the Earth's atmosphere. Most meteoroids burn up in the atmosphere before reaching altitudes of 80 km. A meteor is the streak of light from a meteoroid in the Earth's atmosphere, and is also known as a shooting star. Meteor showers are associated with comets, happen when the Earth passes through the debris of a comet, and are associated with a higher than normal number of meteors. Meteorites are rocks that reach the Earth's surface from space. Fireballs are very bright meteors with trails that can last as long as 30 minutes. A bolide is a fireball that burns up when it enters Earth's atmosphere. There are many types of meteorites, and they are known to be composed of various materials. Iron meteorites consist of iron and nickel with a criss-cross, or Widmanstatten, internal metallic crystalline structure. Stony iron meteorites are composed of iron, nickel, and silicate materials. Stony meteorites consist mainly of silicate and also contain iron and nickel.

Comets

A comet consists of frozen gases and rocky and metallic materials. Comets are usually small and typically have long tails. A comet's tail is made of ionized gases. It points away from the Sun and follows the comet as it approaches the Sun. The tail precedes the head as the comet moves away from the Sun. It is believed that as many as 100 billion comets exist. About 12 new ones are discovered each year. Their orbits are elliptical, not round. Some scientists theorize that short-period comets originate from the Kuiper Belt and long-period comets originate from the Oort Cloud, which is thought to be 100,000 AU away. Comets orbit the Sun in time periods varying from a few years to hundreds of thousands of years. A well-known comet, Halley's Comet, has an orbit of 76 years. It is 80 percent water, and consists of frozen water, carbon dioxide (dry ice), ammonia, and methane.

Earth-Moon-Sun system

The Earth-Moon-Sun system is responsible for eclipses. From Earth, the Sun and the Moon appear to be about the same size. An eclipse of the Sun occurs during a new Moon, when the side of the Moon facing the Earth is not illuminated. The Moon passes in front of the Sun and blocks its view from Earth. Eclipses do not occur every month because the orbit of the Moon is at about a 5° angle to the plane of Earth's orbit. An eclipse of the Moon happens during the full Moon phase. The Moon passes through the shadow of the Earth and blocks sunlight from reaching it, which temporarily causes darkness. During a lunar eclipse, there are two parts to the shadow. The umbra is the dark, inner region. The sun is completely blocked in this area. The penumbra is a partially lighted area around the umbra. Earth's shadow is four times longer than the Moon's shadow.

Natural satellites

There are about 335 moons, or satellites, that orbit the planets and objects in the solar system. Many of these satellites have been recently discovered, a few are theoretical, some are asteroid moons (moons orbiting asteroids), some are moonlets (small moons), and some are moons of dwarf planets and objects that have not been definitively categorized, such as trans-Neptunian objects. Mercury and Venus do not have any moons. There are several moons larger than the dwarf planet Pluto and two larger than Mercury. Some consider the Earth and Moon a pair of double planets rather than a planet and a satellite.

- 95 -

Some satellites may have started out as asteroids. They were eventually captured by a planet's gravity and became moons.

Remote sensing

Remote sensing refers to the gathering of data about an object or phenomenon without physical or intimate contact with the object being studied. The data can be viewed or recorded and stored in many forms (visually with a camera, audibly, or in the form of data). Gathering weather data from a ship, satellite, or buoy might be thought of as remote sensing. The monitoring of a fetus through the use of ultrasound technology provides a remote image. Listening to the heartbeat of a fetus is another example of remote sensing. Methods for remote sensing can be grouped as radiometric, geodetic, or acoustic. Examples of radiometric remote sensing include radar, laser altimeters, light detection and ranging (LIDAR) used to determine the concentration of chemicals in the air, and radiometers used to detect various frequencies of radiation. Geodetic remote sensing involves measuring the small fluctuations in Earth's gravitational field. Examples of acoustic remote sensing include underwater sonar and seismographs.

Phases of the Moon

It takes about one month for the Moon to go through all its phases. Waxing refers to the two weeks during which the Moon goes from a new moon to a full moon. About two weeks is spent waning, going from a full moon to a new moon. The lit part of the Moon always faces the Sun. The phases of waxing are: new moon, during which the Moon is not illuminated and rises and sets with the Sun; crescent moon, during which a tiny sliver is lit; first quarter, during which half the Moon is lit and the phase of the Moon is due south on the meridian; gibbous, during which more than half of the Moon is lit and has a shape similar to a football; right side, during which the Moon is lit; and full moon, during which the Moon is fully illuminated, rises at sunset, and sets at sunrise. After a full moon, the Moon is waning. The phases of waning are: gibbous, during which the left side is lit and the Moon rises after sunset and sets after sunrise; third quarter, during which the Moon is half lit and rises at midnight and sets at noon; crescent, during which a tiny sliver is lit; and new moon, during which the Moon is not illuminated and rises and sets with the Sun.

Tropic of Cancer, Tropic of Capricorn; Antarctic and Arctic Circles

Tropic of Cancer: This is located at 23.5 degrees north. The Sun is directly overhead at noon on June 21st in the Tropic of Cancer, which marks the beginning of summer in the Northern Hemisphere.

Tropic of Capricorn: This is located at 23.5 degrees south. The Sun is directly overhead at noon on December 21st in the Tropic of Capricorn, which marks the beginning of winter in the Northern Hemisphere.

Arctic Circle: This is located at 66.5 degrees north, and marks the start of when the Sun is not visible above the horizon. This occurs on December 21st, the same day the Sun is directly over the Tropic of Capricorn.

Antarctic Circle: This is located at 66.5 degrees south, and marks the start of when the Sun is not visible above the horizon. This occurs on June 21st, which marks the beginning of winter in the Southern Hemisphere and is when the Sun is directly over the Tropic of Cancer.

Latitude, longitude, and equator

For the purposes of tracking time and location, the Earth is divided into sections with imaginary lines. Lines that run vertically around the globe through the poles are lines of longitude, sometimes called meridians. The Prime Meridian is the longitudinal reference point of 0. Longitude is measured in 15-degree increments toward the east or west. Degrees are further divided into 60 minutes, and each minute is divided into 60 seconds. Lines of latitude run horizontally around the Earth parallel to the equator, which is the 0 reference point and the widest point of the Earth. Latitude is the distance north or south from the equator, and is also measured in degrees, minutes, and seconds.

Geosynchronous and geostationary orbits

A geosynchronous orbit around the Earth has an orbital period matching the Earth's sidereal rotation period. Sidereal rotation is based on the position of a fixed star, not the Sun, so a sidereal day is slightly shorter than a 24-hour solar day. A satellite in a geosynchronous orbit appears in the same place in the sky at the same time each day. Technically, any object with an orbit time period equal to the Earth's rotational period is geosynchronous. A geostationary orbit is a geosynchronous orbit that is circular and at zero inclination, which means the object is located directly above the equator. Geostationary orbits are useful for communications satellites because they are fixed in the same spot relative to the Earth. A semisynchronous orbit has an orbital period of half a sidereal day.

Equinox, solstice, perihelion, and aphelion

Equinox: This occurs twice each year when the Sun crosses the plane of the Earth's celestial equator. During an equinox, Earth is not tilted away from or towards the Sun. The length of day and night are roughly equal. The two equinoxes are the March equinox and the September equinox.

Solstice: The summer solstice, the day with the most amount of sunlight, occurs on June 21st in the Northern Hemisphere and on December 21st in the Southern Hemisphere. The winter solstice, the day with the least amount of sunlight, occurs on December 21st in the Northern Hemisphere and on June 21st in the Southern Hemisphere.

Perihelion: This is the point in an object's orbit when it is closest to the Sun.

Aphelion: This is the point in an object's orbit when it is farthest from the Sun.

Piloted space missions

The Soviet space program successfully completed the first space flight by orbiting Yuri Gagarin in 1961 on Vostok 1. His orbit lasted 1 hour, 48 minutes. Later in 1961, the U.S. completed its first piloted space flight by launching Alan Shepard into space in the Mercury-Redstone 3. This space mission was suborbital. The first woman in space was Valentina Tereshkova, who orbited the Earth 48 times aboard Vostok 6 in 1963. The first space flight with more than one person and also the first that didn't involve space suits took place on the Voskhod in 1964. The first person on the Moon was American Neil Armstrong. In 1969, he traveled to the Moon on Apollo 11, which was the 11th manned space flight completed in the Apollo program, which was conducted from 1968 to 1972. In 2003, Yang Liwei became the first person from China to go into space. He traveled onboard the Shenzhou 5. The Space Shuttle Orbiter has included piloted space shuttles from 1981 until the present. The program was suspended after two space shuttle disasters: Challenger in 1986 and Columbia in 2003.

Notable satellites

The first satellite to orbit the Earth was the Soviet Union's Sputnik 1 in 1957. Its two radio transmitters emitted beeps that were received by radios around the world. Analysis of the radio signals was used to gather information about the electron density of the ionosphere. Soviet success escalated the American space program. In 1958, the U.S. put Explorer 1 into orbit. The Osumi was the first Japanese satellite, which was put into orbit in 1970. The Vanguard 1 is the satellite that has orbited the Earth the longest. It was put into orbit in 1958 and was still in orbit in June, 2009. The Mir Space Station orbited Earth for 11 years, and was assembled in space starting in 1986. It was almost continuously occupied until 1999. The International Space Station began being assembled in orbit in 1998. At 43,000 cubic feet, it is the largest manned object sent into space. It circles the Earth every 90 minutes.

Limitations of space exploration

There are many limitations of space exploration. The main limitation is knowledge. Space exploration is currently time-consuming, dangerous, and costly. Manned and unmanned missions, even within the solar system, take years of planning and years to complete. The associated financial costs are great. Interstellar travel and intergalactic is not yet realistically feasible. Technological advances are needed before these types of missions can be carried out. By some estimates, it would take more than 70 years to travel to Proxima Centauri (the nearest star) using the fastest rocket technology available. It would take much longer using less advanced technologies. Space travel is dangerous for many reasons. Rocket fuel is highly explosive. Non-Earth environments are uninhabitable for humans. Finally, astronauts are exposed to larger than usual amounts of radiation.

Unpiloted space missions

The first artificial object to reach another space object was Luna 2. It crashed on the Moon in 1959. The first automatic landing was by Luna 9. It landed on the Moon in 1966. Mariner 2's flyby of Venus in 1962 was the first successful interplanetary flyby. Venera 7 landing on and transmitting data from Venus was the first interplanetary surface landing, which took place in 1970. The first soft landing on Mars was in 1971. Unpiloted spacecraft have also made successful soft landings on the asteroids Eros and Itokawa, as well as Titan, a moon of Saturn. The first flyby of Jupiter was in 1973 by Pioneer 10. Pioneer 10 was also the first craft of its kind to leave the solar system. The first flyby of Mercury was in 1974 by Mariner. The first flyby of Saturn was in 1979 by Pioneer 11. The first flyby of Uranus was in 1986 by Voyager 2, which also flew by Neptune in 1989.

Granite and basalt

Both granite and basalt are plentiful igneous rocks, but granite is intrusive and basalt is extrusive. Intrusive rocks come from magma within the Earth's crust and cool slowly. Extrusive rocks are formed from lava on the Earth's surface and cool more quickly than intrusive rocks. Granite is an igneous rock with a medium to coarse texture that is formed from magma. It can be a variety of colors. It is intrusive, massive, hard, and coarse grained. It forms a major part of continental crust. It can be composed of potassium feldspar, plagioclase feldspar, and quartz, as well as various amounts of muscovite, biotite, and hornblende-type amphiboles. Basalt is extrusive and usually colored gray to black. It has a fine grain due to quicker cooling. Basalt is porphyritic, meaning it contains larger crystals in a fine matrix. Basalt is usually composed of amphibole and pyroxene, and sometimes of plagioclase, feldspathoids, and olivine.

Moon facts

The Moon is the fifth largest satellite in the solar system. It orbits the Earth about every 27.3 days. The changes of the Earth, Sun, and Moon in relation to each other cause the phases of the Moon, which repeat every 29.5 days. The Moon's gravitational pull (along with the Sun's) is responsible for the tides on Earth. Its diameter is about 3,474 km and its gravity is about 17% of Earth's. The lunar maria (plural of mare) on the Moon's surface is dark thin layers composed of dark basalt. They were formed by ancient volcanoes. There are many impact craters on the Moon. There were numerous impact craters on Earth at one time, but they have been transformed by erosion over time. Very few are still visible.

Matter, Structure, and Practical Knowledge

Pure substances

Pure substances are substances that cannot be further broken down into simpler substances and still retain their characteristics. Pure substances are categorized as either elements or compounds. Elements that consist of only one type of atom may be monatomic, diatomic, or polyatomic. For example, helium (He) and copper (Cu) are monatomic elements, and hydrogen (H_2) and oxygen (O_2) are diatomic elements. Phosphorus (P_4) and sulfur (S_8) are polyatomic elements. Compounds consist of molecules of more than one type of atom. For example, pure water (H_2O) is made up of molecules consisting of two atoms of hydrogen bonded to one atom of oxygen, and glucose ($C_6H_{12}O_6$) is made up of molecules of six carbon atoms and twelve hydrogen atoms bonded together with six oxygen atoms.

Mixtures

Mixtures can be classified as either homogeneous mixtures or heterogeneous mixtures. The molecules of homogeneous mixtures are distributed uniformly throughout the mixture, but the molecules of heterogeneous mixtures are not distributed uniformly throughout the mixture. Air is an example of a homogeneous mixture, and a pile of sand and rock is an example of a heterogeneous mixture. Solutions are homogeneous mixtures consisting of a solute (the substance that is dissolved) and a solvent (the substance doing the dissolving).

Suspensions

Suspensions are heterogeneous mixtures in which the particle size of the substance suspended is too large to be kept in suspension by Brownian motion. Once left undisturbed, suspensions will settle out to form layers. An example of a suspension is sand stirred into water. Left undisturbed, the sand will fall out of suspension and the water will form a layer on top of the sand.

Atoms and molecules

Atoms are the smallest particles of an element that still retain the properties of that element. Molecules are made of two or more atoms. Molecules are the smallest particles of a compound that still retain the properties of that compound. For example, water molecules contain two hydrogen atoms covalently bonded to one oxygen atom. Also, elements may be diatomic or polyatomic molecules. For example, hydrogen gas (H_2) exists naturally as diatomic molecules.

Chemical and physical properties

Matter has both physical and chemical properties. Physical properties can be seen or observed without changing the identity or composition of matter. For example, the mass, volume, and density of a substance can be determined without permanently changing the sample. Other physical properties include color, boiling point, freezing point, solubility, odor, hardness, electrical conductivity, thermal conductivity, ductility, and malleability.

Chemical properties cannot be measured without changing the identity or composition of matter. Chemical properties describe how a substance reacts or changes to form a new substance. Examples of chemical properties include flammability, corrosivity, oxidation states, enthalpy of formation, and reactivity with other chemicals.

Chemical and physical changes

Physical changes do not produce new substances. The atoms or molecules may be rearranged, but no new substances are formed. Phase changes or changes of state such as melting, freezing, and sublimation are physical changes. For example, physical changes include the melting of ice, the boiling of water, sugar dissolving into water, and the crushing of a piece of chalk into a fine powder.

Chemical changes involve a chemical reaction and do produce new substances. When iron rusts, iron oxide is formed, indicating a chemical change. Other examples of chemical changes include baking a cake, burning wood, digesting food, and mixing an acid and a base.

Intensive and extensive properties

Physical properties are categorized as either intensive or extensive. Intensive properties *do not* depend on the amount of matter or quantity of the sample. This means that intensive properties will not change if the sample size is increased or decreased. Intensive properties include color, hardness, melting point, boiling point, density, ductility, malleability, specific heat, temperature, concentration, and magnetization.

Extensive properties *do* depend on the amount of matter or quantity of the sample. Therefore, extensive properties do change if the sample size is increased or decreased. If the sample size is increased, the property increases. If the sample size is decreased, the property decreases. Extensive properties include volume, mass, weight, energy, entropy, number of moles, and electrical charge.

States of matter

The four states of matter are solids, liquids, gases, and plasma. Solids have a definite shape and a definite volume. Because solid particles are held in fairly rigid positions, solids are the least compressible of the four states of matter. Liquids have definite volumes but no definite shapes. Because their particles are free to slip and slide over each other, liquids take the shape of their containers, but they still remain fairly incompressible by natural means. Gases have no definite shape or volume. Because gas particles are free to move, they move away from each other to fill their containers. Gases are compressible. Plasmas are high-temperature, ionized gases that exist only under very high temperatures at which electrons are stripped away from their atoms.

Atomic properties of neutral atoms, anions, and cations

Neutral atoms have equal numbers of protons and electrons. Cations are positively-charged ions that are formed when atoms lose electrons in order to have a full outer shell of valence electrons. For example, the alkali metals sodium and potassium form the cations Na^+ and K^+, and the alkaline earth metals magnesium and calcium form the cations Mg^{2+} and Ca^{2+}.

Anions are negatively-charged ions that are formed when atoms gain electrons to fill their outer shell of valence electrons. For example, the halogens fluorine and chlorine form the anions F⁻ and Cl⁻.

Law of conservation of energy

The law of conservation of energy states that in a closed system, energy cannot be created or destroyed but only changed from one form to another. This is also known as the first law of thermodynamics. Another way to state this is that the total energy in an isolated system is constant. Energy comes in many forms that may be transformed from one kind to another, but in a closed system, the total amount of energy is conserved or remains constant. For example, potential energy can be converted to kinetic energy, thermal energy, radiant energy, or mechanical energy. In an isolated chemical reaction, there can be no energy created or destroyed. The energy simply changes forms.

Law of conservation of mass

The law of conservation of mass is also known as the law of conservation of matter. This basically means that in a closed system, the total mass of the products must equal the total mass of the reactants. This could also be stated that in a closed system, mass never changes. A consequence of this law is that matter is never created or destroyed during a typical chemical reaction. The atoms of the reactants are simply rearranged to form the products. The number and type of each specific atom involved in the reactants is identical to the number and type of atoms in the products. This is the key principle used when balancing chemical equations. In a balanced chemical equation, the number of moles of each element on the reactant side equals the number of moles of each element on the product side.

Kinetic and potential energy

The internal energy of a system may be categorized as kinetic energy or potential energy. Kinetic energy is the energy of a system associated with movement. In chemical systems, this movement is predicted by the kinetic theory of matter and is due to the random movement of the particles that make up the system. The kinetic energy of a particle may be calculated by the following formula: $KE = \frac{1}{2}mv^2$, where KE is the kinetic energy in joules, m is the mass of the particle in kilograms, and v is the velocity of the particle in meters per second.

Potential energy is the stored energy in a system associated with position or configuration. In chemical systems, this energy is the energy associated with the chemical bonds and intermolecular forces of the matter contained in the system.

Chemical, electrical, electromagnetic, nuclear, and thermal energy

Different types of energy may be associated with systems:
- Chemical energy is the energy that is stored in chemical bonds and intermolecular forces.
- Electrical energy is the energy associated with the movement of electrons or ions through a material.

- 102 -

- Electromagnetic energy is the energy of electromagnetic waves of several frequencies including radio waves, microwaves, infrared light, visible light, ultraviolet light, x-rays, and gamma rays.
- Nuclear energy is the binding energy that is stored within an atom's nucleus.
- Thermal energy is the total internal kinetic energy of a system due to the random motions of the particles.

Conversion of energy within chemical systems

Chemical energy is the energy stored in molecules in the bonds between the atoms of those molecules and the energy associated with the intermolecular forces. This stored potential energy may be converted into kinetic energy and then into heat. During a chemical reaction, atoms may be rearranged and chemical bonds may be formed or broken accompanied by a corresponding absorption or release of energy, usually in the form of heat. According to the first law of thermodynamics, during these energy conversions, the total amount of energy must be conserved.

Groups and periods in the periodic table

A group is a vertical column of the periodic table. Elements in the same group have the same number of valence electrons. For the representative elements, the number of valence electrons is equal to the group number. Because of their equal valence electrons, elements in the same groups have similar physical and chemical properties. A period is a horizontal row of the periodic table. Atomic number increases from left to right across a row. The period of an element corresponds to the highest energy level of the electrons in the atoms of that element. The energy level increases from top to bottom down a group.

Atomic number and atomic mass in the periodic table

The elements in the periodic table are arranged in order of increasing atomic number first left to right and then top to bottom across the periodic table. The atomic number represents the number of protons in the atoms of that element. Because of the increasing numbers of protons, the atomic mass typically also increases from left to right across a period and from top to bottom down a row. The atomic mass is a weighted average of all the naturally occurring isotopes of an element.

Atomic symbols

The atomic symbol for many elements is simply the first letter of the element name. For example, the atomic symbol for hydrogen is H, and the atomic symbol for carbon is C. The atomic symbol of other elements is the first two letters of the element name. For example, the atomic symbol for helium is He, and the atomic symbol for cobalt is Co. The atomic symbols of several elements are derived from Latin. For example, the atomic symbol for copper (Cu) is derived from *cuprum,* and the atomic symbol for iron (Fe) is derived from *ferrum.* The atomic symbol for tungsten (W) is derived from the German word *wolfram.*

Arrangement of metals, nonmetals, and metalloids in the periodic table

The metals are located on the left side and center of the periodic table, and the nonmetals are located on the right side of the periodic table. The metalloids or semimetals form a zigzag line between the metals and nonmetals as shown below. Metals include the alkali metals such as lithium, sodium, and potassium and the alkaline earth metals such as beryllium, magnesium, and calcium. Metals also include the transition metals such as iron, copper, and nickel and the inner transition metals such as thorium, uranium, and plutonium. Nonmetals include the chalcogens such as oxygen and sulfur, the halogens such as fluorine and chlorine, and the noble gases such as helium and argon. Carbon, nitrogen, and phosphorus are also nonmetals. Metalloids or semimetals include boron, silicon, germanium, antimony, and polonium.

Arrangement of transition elements

The transition elements belong to one of two categories—transition metals or inner transition metals. The transition metals are located in the middle of the periodic table, and the inner transition metals are typically set off as two rows by themselves at the bottom of the periodic table. The transition metals correspond to the "*d* block" for orbital filling, and the inner transition metals correspond to the "*f* block" for orbital filling. Examples of transition metals include iron, copper, nickel, and zinc. The inner transition metals consist of the *lanthanide* or *rare-earth series*, which corresponds to the first row, and the *actinide series*, which corresponds to the second row of the inner transition metals. The *lanthanide series* includes lanthanum, cerium, and praseodymium. The *actinide series* includes actinium, uranium, and plutonium.

Periodic trends

Atomic radius size
Atomic radius size decreases across a period from left to right and increases down a group from top to bottom. The atomic radius decreases across a period due to the increasing number of protons and the attraction between those protons and the orbiting electrons. The atomic radius increases down a group due to the increasing energy levels. Atoms in the top-right corner of the periodic table (including hydrogen) have the smallest atomic radii, and atoms in the bottom-left corner of the periodic table have the largest atomic radii. Helium has the smallest atomic radius, and cesium has the largest confirmed atomic radius.

Ionic radius size
The ionic radius size increases down a group of the periodic table. This is due to the increasing energy levels and the fact that electrons are orbiting farther and farther from the nucleus. The trend seen across the periods of the periodic table is due to the formation of cations or anions. Metals form cations or positive ions. Cations are smaller than their

neutral atoms due to the loss of one or more electrons. Nonmetals except the noble gases form anions or negative ions. Anions are larger than their neutral atoms due to the gain of one or more electrons.

Ionization energy

Ionization energy is the amount of energy needed to remove an electron from an isolated atom. Ionization energy decreases down a group of the periodic table because the electrons get farther and farther from the nucleus making it easier for the electron to be removed. Ionization energy increases across a period of the periodic table due to the decreasing atomic size, which is due to the increasing number of protons attracting the electrons towards the nucleus. These trends of ionization energy are the opposite of the trends for atomic radius.

Electron affinity

Electron affinity is the energy required to add an electron to a neutral atom in the gaseous phase of an element. If electrons are added to a halogen such as fluorine or chlorine, energy is released and the electron affinity is negative. If electrons are added to an alkaline earth metal, energy is absorbed and the electron affinity is positive. In general, electron affinity becomes more negative from left to right across a period in the periodic table. Electron affinity becomes less negative from the top to the bottom of a group of the periodic table.

Electronegativity

Electronegativity is a measure of the ability of an atom that is chemically combined to at least one other atom in a molecule to attract electrons to it. The Pauling scale is commonly used to assign values to the elements, with fluorine, which is the most electronegative element, being assigned a value of 4.0. Electronegativity increases from left to right across a period of the periodic table and decreases from top to bottom down a group of the periodic table.

Physical properties of the elements in relation to the periodic table

The boiling point, melting point, and conductivity of the elements depend partially on the number of valence electrons of the atoms of those elements. For the representative elements in groups 1A–8A, the number of valence electrons matches the group number. Because all of the elements in each individual group contain the same number of valence electrons, elements in the same groups tend to have similar boiling points, melting points, and conductivity. Boiling points and melting points tend to decrease moving down the column of groups 1A–4A and 8A but increase slightly moving down the column of groups 5A–7A.

Chemical reactivity in relation to the periodic table

Atoms of elements in the same group or family of the periodic table tend to have similar chemical properties and similar chemical reactions. For example, the alkali metals, which form cations with a charge of +1, tend to react with water to form hydrogen gas and metal hydroxides. The alkaline earth metals, which form cations with a charge of +2, react with oxygen gas to form metal oxides. The halogens, which form anions with a charge of −1, are highly reactive and toxic. The noble gases are unreactive and never form compounds naturally.

Protons, neutrons, and electrons

The three major subatomic particles are the proton, neutron, and electron. The proton, which is located in the nucleus, has a relative charge of +1. The neutron, which is located in the nucleus, has a relative charge of 0. The electron, which is located outside the nucleus, has a relative charge of –1. The proton and neutron, which are essentially the same mass, are much more massive than the electron and make up the mass of the atom. The electron's mass is insignificant compared to the mass of the proton and neutron.

Orbits and orbitals

An orbit is a definite path, but an orbital is a region in space. The Bohr model described electrons as orbiting or following a definite path in space around the nucleus of an atom. But, according to Heisenberg's uncertainty principle, it is impossible to determine the location and the momentum of an electron simultaneously. Therefore, it is impossible to draw a definite path or orbit of an electron. An orbital as described by the quantum-mechanical model or the electron-cloud model is a region in space that is drawn in such a way as to indicate the probability of finding an electron at a specific location. The distance an orbital is located from the nucleus corresponds to the principal quantum number. The orbital shape corresponds to the subshell or azimuthal quantum number. The orbital orientation corresponds to the magnetic quantum number.

Quantum numbers

The principal quantum number (n) describes an electron's shell or energy level and actually describes the size of the orbital. Electrons farther from the nucleus are at higher energy levels. The subshell or azimuthal quantum number (l) describes the electron's sublevel or subshell (s, p, d, or f) and specifies the shape of the orbital. Typical shapes include spherical, dumbbell, and clover leaf. The magnetic quantum number (m_l) describes the orientation of the orbital in space. The spin or magnetic moment quantum number (m_s) describes the direction of the spin of the electron in the orbital.

Atomic number and mass number

The atomic number of an element is the number of protons in the nucleus of an atom of that element. This is the number that identifies the type of an atom. For example, all oxygen atoms have eight protons, and all carbon atoms have six protons. Each element is identified by its specific atomic number.

The mass number is the number of protons and neutrons in the nucleus of an atom. Although the atomic number is the same for all atoms of a specific element, the mass number can vary due to the varying numbers of neutrons in various isotopes of the atom.

Isotopes

Isotopes are atoms of the same element that vary in their number of neutrons. Isotopes of the same element have the same number of protons and thus the same atomic number. But, because isotopes vary in the number of neutrons, they can be identified by their mass numbers. For example, two naturally occurring carbon isotopes are carbon-12 and carbon-13, which have mass numbers 12 and 13, respectively. The symbols $^{12}_{6}C$ and $^{13}_{6}C$ also represent the carbon isotopes. The general form of the symbol is $_A^M X$, where X represents the element symbol, M represents the mass number, and A represents the atomic number.

Average atomic mass

The *average atomic mass* is the weighted average of the masses of all the naturally occurring isotopes of an atom in comparison to the carbon-12 isotope. The unit for average atomic mass is the atomic mass unit (u). Atomic masses of isotopes are measured using a mass spectrometer by bombarding a gaseous sample of the isotope and measuring its relative deflections. Atomic masses can be calculated if the percent abundances and the atomic masses of the naturally occurring isotopes are known.

Aufbau principle

The *Aufbau principle* is named from the German word for "building up," and it describes how electrons fill the energy levels or shells of an atom. In general, electrons will fill the $n = 1$ energy level before filling the $n = 2$ energy level, and electrons will fill the $n = 2$ energy level before filling the $n = 3$ energy level. The s subshell of an energy level will fill before the p subshell, which fills before the d and f subshells.

Hund's rule

Hund's rule describes how electrons fill the orbitals in a sublevel. Less energy is required for an electron to occupy an orbital alone than the energy needed for an electron to pair up with another electron in an orbital. Therefore, electrons will occupy each orbital in a subshell before electrons will begin to pair up in those orbitals. For example, in the $2p$ subshell, one electron will occupy each of the three orbitals before pairing begins. In the $3d$ subshell, one electron will occupy each of the five orbitals before pairing begins.

Pauli exclusion principle

The *Pauli exclusion principle* describes the unique address or location of each electron in an atom. Each electron has a unique or exclusive set of four quantum numbers indicating the electron's energy level, subshell, orbital orientation, and magnetic moment. Every orbital can hold a maximum of two electrons, but even if two electrons occupy the same orbital resulting in identical energy levels, subshells, and orbital orientations, they must have opposite spins, which means that their magnetic moment quantum numbers will differ.

Correlation between the electron configuration and the periodic table

Electron configurations show a direct correlation to the periodic table. The periodic table can be divided into blocks representing *s, p, d,* and *f* subshells. The energy level corresponds to the row or period of the periodic table. The subshells, *s, p, d,* or *f* are related to the block's group numbers. The *s* block corresponds to groups 1A and 2A. The *p* block corresponds to groups 3A–8A. The *d* block corresponds to the 10 groups of transition metals, and the *f* block corresponds to the two rows of inner transition metals (14 groups) located at the bottom of the table.

Electron configuration

The chemical and physical properties of atoms are related to the number of valence electrons the atom possesses. Atoms (except hydrogen and helium) seek to have eight electrons in their outer shell as stated in the octet rule. A full octet corresponds to full *s* and *p* orbitals. Noble gases have full *s* and *p* orbitals and are inert. To fulfill the octet rule, elements in groups 1A (alkali metals) and 2A (alkaline earth metals) tend to lose one or two electrons, respectively, forming cations. Elements in group 6A (chalcogens) and group 7A (halogens) tend to gain one or two electrons, respectively, forming anions. Other elements such as carbon (group 4A) tend to form covalent bonds to satisfy the octet rule.

Cathode ray tube (CRT)

Electrons were discovered by Joseph John Thomson through scientific work with cathode ray tubes (CRTs). Cathode rays had been studied for many years, but it was Thomson who showed that cathode rays were negatively charged particles. Although Thomson could not determine an electron's charge or mass, he was able to determine the ratio of the charge to the mass. Thomson discovered that this ratio was constant regardless of the gas in the CRT. He was able to show that the cathode rays were actually streams of negatively charged particles by deflecting them with a positively charged plate.